Robert D. Gilbreath

FORWARD
THINKING

Forward Thinking

The Pragmatist's Guide to Today's Business Trends

Robert D. Gilbreath

Understanding change is not enough.
You must learn to survive it, exploit it,
and profit from it.

McGraw-Hill Book Company

New York St. Louis San Francisco Auckland Bogotá
Hamburg Johannesburg London Madrid Mexico
Milan Montreal New Delhi Panama
Paris São Paulo Singapore
Sydney Tokyo Toronto

Library of Congress Cataloging-in-Publication Data

Gilbreath, Robert D. (Robert Dean), date.
  Forward thinking.

  Bibliography: p.
  Includes index.
  1. Industrial management.   2. Organizational
change.   I. Title.
HD31.G496   1987   658.4   86-27732
ISBN 0-07-023262-8

Copyright© 1987 by Robert D. Gilbreath. All rights reserved.
Printed in the United States of America. Except as permitted
under the United States Copyright Act of 1976, no part of this
publication may be reproduced or distributed in any form or by
any means, or stored in a data base or retrieval system, without
the prior written permission of the publisher.

1234567890   DOC/DOC   8932109876

ISBN 0-07-023262-8

The editors for this book were William A. Sabin and Georgia Kornbluth,
the designer was Naomi Auerbach, and the production supervisor
was Thomas G. Kowalczyk. It was set in Baskerville by Harper Graphics Inc.

Printed and bound by R. R. Donnelley & Sons Company

*For Linda, a wonderful partner
in the ever-changing dance of life.*

Permission to reprint excerpts from the following publications is gratefully acknowledged.

The Affluent Society by John Kenneth Galbraith, reprinted by permission of Houghton Mifflin Company. Copyright 1958, 1969, 1976 by John Kenneth Galbraith.

"Among School Children," by William Butler Yeats, from *Immortal Poems of the English Language*, Oscar Williams (ed.), Washington Square Press, reprinted by permission of Macmillan Publishing Company. Copyright 1928 by Macmillan Publishing Company, renewed 1956 by Georgie Yeats.

The Aquarian Conspiracy by Marilyn Ferguson, reprinted by permission of Jeremy P. Tarcher, Inc. Copyright 1980 by Marilyn Ferguson.

"Autonomy," from *The Lives of a Cell* by Lewis Thomas, reprinted by permission of Viking Penguin, Inc. Originally published in the *New England Journal of Medicine*. Copyright 1972 by the Massachusetts Medical Society.

Bergson and the Evolution of Physics by P. A. Y. Gunter, reprinted by permission of the University of Tennessee Press.

"Bird and the Machine," from *The Star Thrower* by Loren Eiseley, reprinted by permission of Random House, Inc. Copyright 1955 by Loren Eiseley.

The Challenge of Hidden Profits by Mark Green and John F. Berry, reprinted by permission of William Morrow and Company, Inc. Copyright 1985 by Mark Green and John F. Berry.

The Discoverers: A History of Man's Search to Know His World and Himself by Daniel J. Boorstin, reprinted by permission of Random House, Inc. Copyright 1983 by Daniel J. Boorstin.

Entrophy: A New World View by Jeremy Rifkin with Ted Howard, reprinted by Viking Penguin, Inc. Copyright 1980 by the Foundation on Economic Trends.

Honoring the Self by Nathaniel Branden, reprinted by permission of Nathaniel Branden. Copyright 1983 by Nathaniel Branden.

In Search of Excellence—Lessons from America's Best-Run Companies by Thomas J. Peters and Robert H. Waterman Jr., reprinted by permission of Harper & Row Publishers, Inc. Copyright 1982 by Thomas J. Peters and Robert H. Waterman, Jr.

The Last Unicorn by Peter S. Beagle, reprinted by permission of Viking Penguin, Inc. Copyright 1980 by Peter S. Beagle.

Manufacturing: The Formidable Competitive Weapon by Wickham Skinner, reprinted by permission of John Wiley & Sons, Inc. Copyright 1985 by John Wiley & Sons, Inc.

Megatrends by John Naisbitt, reprinted by permission of Warner Books, Inc. Copyright 1982 by John Naisbitt.

The New Competitors by D. Quinn Mills, reprinted by permission of John Wiley & Sons, Inc. Copyright 1985 by D. Quinn Mills.

The Reenchantment of the World by Morris Berman, reprinted by permission of Cornell University Press. Copyright 1981 by Morris Berman.

The Sane Society by Erich Fromm, reprinted by permission of Holt, Rinehart and Winston, Inc. Copyright 1955 by Erich Fromm.

"The Star Thrower," from *The Unexpected Universe* by Loren Eiseley, reprinted by permission of Harcourt Brace Jovanovich, Inc. Copyright 1964, 1969 by Loren Eiseley.

The Story of Philosophy by Will Durant, reprinted by permission of Simon and Schuster, Inc. Copyright 1926, 1927, 1933 by Will Durant. Copyright renewed 1954, 1955, 1961 by Will Durant.

The Third Wave by Alvin Toffler, reprinted by permission of William Morrow and Company, Inc. Copyright 1980 by Alvin Toffler.

Walden by Henry David Thoreau, reprinted by permission of New American Library.

Contents

Preface

Any business leader who isn't feeling the earth move beneath his or her feet is living in the past and unprepared for the future. We are now experiencing dynamic differences in every aspect of commercial enterprise—differences that affect the continued viability of our companies and our positions within them. And as time passes, these differences are increasing in frequency and intensity to almost seismic proportions. Something unusual, puzzling, and powerful is at work in every industry and every market, and it shows no sign of stopping or even abating its influence. It is the phenomenon of *change*, and it is gaining on us. We need to give it serious attention.

Evidence of change in the business sector surrounds each of us, whatever our industry or role. We see startling technological changes brought about by the microchip, the laser, genetic engineering, and the industrialization of space. Social changes abound, including the dissolution of the nuclear family, the changing roles of women, the aging of our population, the southwestern tilt of people and businesses, the fitness revolution, and the decentralization of institutions. Our economy has been stunned with inflation, deflation, sine-wave oil pricing, up-down interest rates, and a recurring cycle of panic-hope-panic over national deficits. Where is all this taking us?

Depending on which of the many futurists we read, America is becoming a low-technology culture, a society living within the ruins of a decaying physical infrastructure, an island swarming with foreign competitors, a society of participants, a multiple-choice environment, an information colony, a collapsing fiscal nightmare, or a nation experiencing a rebirth of basic ideals and strengths. No matter which of these trends we believe, we must realize that change is *the factor* in our world and that businesses and managers attuned to the phenomenon of change will survive, while those clinging to the nostalgia of fixed constants will be unearthed in the tar pits of our economy in just a few short years.

Because we are living in a vortex of change, we and our companies must synchronize with it, if not our activity at least our methodologies and value systems. Many have done so, in a number of ways. We will look at them here. But not simply individual companies, *entire industries* have been beaten up by change—witness steel, automobiles, oil, computers, and agriculture. Add the intensification of change through deregulation of the airline, trucking, banking, and telecommunications industries. Consider also the rippling and waving of our economy brought about by intermittent and unpredictable tax revisions, monetary policy, and funding vacillations. All these and more factors yet to be mentioned are fueling this conflagration we shall call *businesschange*: the net result of countless dynamic differences impacting the way we work, think, and view ourselves in the context of commercial endeavors.

Businesschange is the force that won't quit, the trend that can't be modeled, the effect unpredicted, and the factor unattended. It is all these and more, a phenomenon that will not be denied or ignored by the business leaders of tomorrow. It is sure to dominate our thoughts about the very nature of management, and to cast doubt on the value of the tools, techniques, and systems we use to achieve it. New value systems and new perspectives are needed. The ground is simply shaking too much and too fast for us to hold on to yesterday.

That we as a society are intrigued by the phenomenon of change is evidenced by the acclaim and acceptance given such books as *Megatrends* by John Naisbitt, *The Third Wave* by Alvin Toffler, and *Entrophy, A New World View* by Jeremy Rifkin with Ted Howard. These are just a few examples of a large group of thoughtful analyses and projections currently being discussed. Although each of these authors holds a particular view of change as a phenomenon and of the effects it is having on our lives, taken as a whole these books serve to heighten our awareness of change as a subject for thought as well as a profound influence on our singular and collective beings.

Here lies the critical difference between those who prophecize about the future and those who capitalize on it. *Astute* people see trends and deduce important messages from them. *Successful* people use these messages as a roadmap to wealth and enrichment. No matter how perceptive and persistent the messages of our business prophets, there is an intuitive gap between what they foresee and how we should respond to it.

The gap between the ongoing transformation of contemporary society and how we should synchronize with it can engulf even the best of us. This book will help you to bridge that gap—to transform change from an interesting phenomenon into a series of signposts leading to a specific destination, rich in personal and corporate rewards.

Dealing with changed business objectives, circumstances, activity, and resources has always been a management challenge and a skill on which we place great value. We now know that another, very different skill is needed: the ability to deal not only with *changed* variables but with *changing* variables—variables in the process of becoming changed, different, and new. Contemporary business leaders must now be able to manage conditions that are in a state of continuous, unpredictable, and non-uniform flux.

Change doesn't occur in discrete chunks, in finite increments which, once they are in place, wait for us to respond, to adjust, and to reestablish our business practices and controls. The phenomenon of change is much too dynamic, indeterminate and, in fact, *alive* to be represented by a mere step function. If this were the case we could simply predict, or guess, what each new set of changed conditions would be once they were in place. We could adjust our management perspectives, realign our management scaffolding, and set about the business of management once change had finished its work.

The problem with such an approach is that change never finishes its work. It doesn't give us time to adjust to new conditions from old ones simply because the concepts of "new" and "old" are misleading in themselves. "Old" and "new" merely represent our artificial method of categorizing what went before as opposed to what exists at the present. But neither what went before nor what exists at any given time is in a fixed state; neither pauses at any point in relation to the other. Change does much more than shuffle the cards in our management game. We cannot play game 1 with an "old" deck and game 2 with a "new" deck. Indeed, we play with a deck while it is *being shuffled*—while it is in motion, in flux. Tomorrow's winners will have to manage on the fly.

The distinction between "change" as a verb rather than a noun—as an impacting force rather than an impact, as a pervasive series of dynamic differences rather than a packaged set of discrete differences separated by time—is crucial to our treatment of change. Change is seen here as a flow of difference, never wholly predictable, never linear, and never at rest. We live and operate businesses in a sea of change, with many currents moving in many directions and affecting our course in myriad ways.

In order to deal with change on this higher level of perception and control, we must recognize change as a phenomenon rather than a distinction among past, present, and future conditions. But a consciousness of change requires even more. It demands acceptance of the fact that, except in very limited, localized activity, we can never purport to *manage* change. Very rarely can we direct, control, or circumvent change itself. We need to understand it, predict its path, and anticipate its effects. In short, we *manage in change* but do not deceive ourselves into thinking we can *manage change*. Properly understood, however, this is a minor admission, for we can thrive in change without creating it. We can profit in change without pushing it.

Because our societies, enterprises, markets, organizations, people, methods, and even objectives are constantly in transition, perhaps now more than ever before, we must begin by elevating our understanding of change as a phenomenon. The first question we will address is, "What is change?" Once we understand what we're up against, we can explore the important impacts of change—what it means to our businesses, our attitudes, our chances of economic success. Included in this book are critical examinations of how we should modify our business identities, approaches, goals, and values as well as particular techniques—the aim and componentry of our management concepts and our managerial apparatus.

The world of businesschange is as enchanting as it is rational. And attempts to describe it are initially frustrated by lacks in the business lexicon. We must therefore create our own, pragmatic terminology. In this book you will encounter *soft properties, change recalcitrants, immune designs, squealing variables, change targets* and *change shields,* the concepts of *sacrifice* and *hardening, feral change, pivoting managers, compliance drones, specialty transcendence, nurturing cultures* and *extractive cultures, human transducers, listening nets, sensitivity ruts,* and the notion of *pulsework.*

Whatever words we use and whatever metaphors we employ are only secondary in importance. Our primary goal is to make sense of what we know about change and to put that knowledge to work. That's the ultimate challenge of today and tomorrow. Those who accept it will be the leaders of the impending management revolution, confident among the landscapes of the future—the leaders who will create the lessons for the rest, who are certain to follow.

ROBERT D. GILBREATH
Norcross, Georgia

1

Meeting the Challenge of Change

Knowing what you're up against

In modern terms, the dance of contingency,
of the indeterminable outwits us all.
                    LOREN EISELEY

How can we know the dancer from the
dance?
        WILLIAM BUTLER YEATS

Let's attack the notion of change head-on. You don't need to know more about change unless that knowledge leads to survival or exploitation of the phenomenon. But before you can presume to manage in a sea of change, or better yet, to profit through it, you need a firm, pragmatic comprehension of what you're up against—what it is and how it acts.

There are four levels of reaction to change:

1. Ignorance

2. Recognition

3. Accommodation

4. Control

The goal of any sensible business person is to move quickly from position 1 to position 4 on this list. Recognition is preferable to ignorance only insofar as it leads to accommodation or control. Seeing change without being able to ride with it or drive it your own way is much like seeing a speeding truck bearing down upon you as you stand at an intersection— it serves only to heighten your anxiety before you're struck down.

For some changes the most we can hope for is accommodation, but for a surprising many we should and can steer the phenomenon to the destination of our choice—commerical success. We study change in this chapter not just to recognize it but to ride with it or drive it. We must confront change to conquer it. Those wanting to profit from today's prophecies need to:

1. Understand change.

2. Understand our limits in surviving or exploiting it.

3. Relate its action to our business situations.

4. Capitalize on the new business cultures it is creating.

A person's perception of change can occur on many different levels and involve many stages of understanding. Like many other concepts, change seems to become more and more abstract the deeper our understanding becomes. Our approach here will be to delve into the concept of change only so deeply as needed to survive it and exploit it in our personal and corporate lives. *We seek an appropriate understanding with direct payoffs*—not a scholarly understanding.

This in mind, we will see that the more elementary or basic our understanding of change as a concept becomes, the more powerful our implementation of ideas based on the concept will be. The more intimate our knowledge of change, the more effectively we will manage in a world dominated by its presence.

We will see why companies and governments are shedding capital investments, redesigning their products and services, and focusing on the results of their work rather than on the work itself. We will understand the new emphasis on generalization among executives, the reason for greater and more sophisticated human development in corporations, and why demands for renewed management proximity are so strong. And we will appreciate the newest management art—listening—and the newest business model—the project. Finally, we will gain insight into how leaders of the future will measure themselves and their companies, how they will think, and what attributes they will value more or value less. These are all significant reactions to the unfolding prophecies all about us—this thing we call "businesschange." But in order to appreciate these reactions more and to cultivate their benefits, we must first appreciate their cause.

Some Important Principles of Change

Were this a book dealing exclusively with the concept of change, its philosophical meaning, its scientific basis, or its various sociological implications, we could afford detailed and scholarly exploration of the phenomenon it represents. Our purpose in studying change is much more direct and pragmatic. By necessity we must partition the abstraction and its study into defined areas, limited not necessarily by the nature of change itself or our innate curiosity about it, but rather by our ability to reduce any understandings thus gained to increased management perception and improved management facility.

To do this, rather than attack the concept as a whole, let's first list some major aspects of change that impact our ability to understand and exploit. Then we can relate this new consciousness of change to our particular business world. Here are the most important change principles every business leader should understand.

Change Principles

1. Change is indeterminate without considering time.
2. Change is subjectively determined, and its impacts are subjectively felt.
3. Change is not easily unitized.
4. Change is nonexistent without effects.
5. Change defies cause-and-effect analysis.
6. Change is not reversible.
7. Change can dilate, contract, and float.
8. Change is a variable.
9. Our ability to perceive change is limited by us.
10. Our ability to manage in change is limited by our ability to perceive it.

Many more principles could be added to this list, and some will be described circumferentially as our discussion of change develops. Aside from a healthy dose of pragmatism—i.e., we care here about change only insofar as it influences our business experience—the reader is also assumed to have felt significant changes in his or her career, so that listing massive change data and proving the existence of change is unnecessary.

We all know that change is upon us, that many things have changed, and that all signs indicate that change will continue on most fronts, impacting our businesses and management methods well into the future. Readers interested in general substantiation of these assessments are referred to the excellent works in the Bibliography at the end of this book, as well as to numerous and continuing articles in business periodicals and daily newspapers, and most important, to individual experience. Our analysis need not be so much "data-extensive" as material to our business objectives and yielding of insight into the commercial context of the change phenomenon. We want to know change so we can profit through it.

Megachange, Macrochange, and Microchange

There are three types of change: (1) *Megachange* deals with massive, widespread shifts (waves) sweeping across our political, social, spiritual, and economic landscapes. (2) *Macrochange* effects managerially significant differences which directly impinge upon our professional lives. (3) *Microchange* involves detailed, fine-tuned modifications important, at least on the surface, to specific businesses or management techniques.

One of many megachanges is the information-based revolution presently overtaking most industrial societies (see Naisbitt, 1982), and another is the increasing depletion of the earth's finite store of material resources (see Rifkin & Howard, 1980). A macrochange is the increased use of specific information-processing technology to manage business efforts, with the personal computer being the most apparent symbol. Finally, a microchange may be the use of fine ceramics to replace steel or petroleum products in automobile production.

No doubt microchanges can have totally unpredictable and widespread impacts on businesses or society as a whole (can cause macrochanges or megachanges). On the other hand, certain industries can thrive even while their managements or methods are oblivious to overwhelming megachanges. These three types of change are linked at times, but their ties are seldom direct or proportional.

Our focus will be on those macrochanges closely associated with commercial impacts. To achieve this focus, however, we must begin on a conceptual basis and work down to more concrete deductions. We must understand what we're up against in order to survive in a future dominated by it. If you can make it over this hurdle of understanding, the tangible lessons of change will flow swiftly and certainly.

Can We Define Change?

The difficulty in defining change is that it cannot be described or understood independently; we must rely on other equally abstract concepts. In particular, we cannot define or understand "change" without simultaneously defining what we call "time." Time and change are so mutually dependent that for our purposes one may not be had, or at least known, without the other. Let's begin by admitting this dependency and moving on. The most basic definition of "change" is:

Change is difference occurring over time.

We know that differences can exist without regard to time. These we call "static differences," and they relate to instantaneous measurements of one object as opposed to others. "Change," on the other hand, can be defined as *dynamic difference*, that which takes place as time passes. This introduces the first principle of change:

1. Change is indeterminate without considering time.
If we understand time we understand change. This will explain the new business urgency, the intense value of timing, and the fleeting nature of tomorrow's opportunities. It demonstrates the wisdom of selecting the expedient method rather than the "best" alternative. To exploit a changing world we must come to grips with the increasingly elusive concept of time.

The elusiveness of time is unfortunate; time is one of the most abstract, difficult-to-grasp concepts over conceived by the human mind. The difficulty was best expressed by Saint Augustine over a millenium and a half ago: "I know what time is, if no one asks me, but if I try to explain it to one who asks me, I no longer know" (Gunter, 1977, p. 63). Since Saint Augustine's time we have added even more wrinkles to the enigma of time, and therefore to change (thanks to the theories of relativity).

Time has always been defined and measured through change. We have used change as the meterstick with which to measure time since our ancestors first noticed the sun crossing the sky and the moon making its periodic journey through the lunar cycle. Time was expressed as so many days (changes in the position of the sun) or months (changes in the position and appearance of the moon). Yearly cycles were synchronized with the planting and harvesting of crops or changes in the sun's elevation. Climatic changes also indicated elapsed time in the hunter-gatherer and agricultural societies preceding our industrial age.

The problem, however, with the measurements of change developed by different societies was that they were not divisible by, invariant from, or synchronized with the measurements used by other peoples encountered or traded with. The need then was to define change (and thus define time), standardize its impacts, and use this standard as a universal measurement to solve these problems. The device that met this need was the *clock*. The value of the clock was that it solved the riddle of time by using change to define its passage (change in the locations of the clock's hands, number of chimes struck, amount of water remaining in a reservoir, etc.). "Time" in this sense is *what it takes for change to occur*.

Time thus became (1) defined, (2) graduated into equal increments (unitized), (3) divisible, (4) uniformly measured, (5) interchangeable, and (6) manageable. The discovery and conquest of time represented a significant accomplishment, best described by Daniel J. Boorstin in his wonderful book *The Discoverers:* "The first great discovery was time, the landscape of experience. . . . Communities of time would bring the first communities of knowledge, ways to share a discovery, a common frontier on the unknown" (1983, p. 1).

Change: A New Riddle

Once time had been conquered and its riddle put to rest, the riddle became change. For if time and change are inseparable and mutually supporting, we cannot fix one without freeing the other. The more defined time becomes, the more abstract change becomes. Change as understood in our culture is even more elusive than time. It is not (1) defined, (2) graduated into equal increments, (3) divisible, (4) uniformly measured, (5) interchangeable, or (6) manageable. One but not both of these variables—time and change—could be nailed down. Time got there first and became firmly established as the dependent variable in the time-change equation.

Can Time Disappear?

Let's illustrate both the anthropocentric characters and the symbiotic identities of time and change. Suppose, for instance, that change disappeared. That is, for some reason and without warning, no changes were permitted. What would this do to our concept of time?

Imagine our world without change. All movement would stop. Birds would halt motionless in the skies. Wind would cease; people would stop moving, breathing, thinking; their hearts would not beat and blood would stop flowing within their veins; clocks would not change (their hands would be stilled). The sun would be fixed in the heavens, no sounds would be heard, no sensations felt. It would be as if some divine power had commanded all things, "Freeze!"

An outside observer witnessing our world from afar would notice that change ceased to exist, that everything was frozen in place, that "time seemed to be standing still." Those of us on earth would sense no change and therefore would be unable to sense the passage of time—or even its existence, for time would not exist without change. Not only would time stand still, it would disappear, existing no longer. Nor would it be missed, for time has meaning as a concept only insofar as we use it to demonstrate or to measure change. Time is indeterminate without considering change. The converse is also true.

2. Change is subjectively determined, with its impacts subjectively felt.

This leads us to devalue incremental measurements of success, specific business plans, generic forecasts, and quantitative analysis. We will feel change and trust our feelings; embrace it rather than analyze it clinically.

Most changes, as opposed to time, are *subjectively* determined. That is, what has changed, by how much, and what such a change means are questions requiring judgment before they can be answered. In the case of a growing child we can quantify change in height and weight fairly objectively, but what about change in posture, gait, dexterity, or even appearance, interests, insight, or ability to love? How are these measured? The detection, assessment, and impact of these changes are functions of the person making, or better, *feeling* them.

Some in the world of business may object to this principle, citing clearly definable and objective indicators of change. For example, they could point to inventories showing more or less stock, sales reports showing more or less revenue, and payroll records showing a higher or lower percentage of overhead composed of officers' salaries. All these are examples of quantifiable differences that may occur over time—yes, changes. We can, however, modify our definition of each, or change the way each is measured *subjectively* and give vastly different results. For example, we could revamp our method of inventory valuation (LIFO, FIFO, etc.) and achieve a different dollar value of stock on hand. We could change our fiscal year and thereby invalidate previous sales figures. Or we could revise our definitions of "overhead" and "salary," and our methods of accounting (pool size, burden allocation, etc.) to arrive at an entirely different percentage of overhead represented by officers' salaries.

In each of these cases, though the method of measurement may be objective (a dollar *is* a dollar, 10 percent *is* 10 percent) the *difference* or the *time* has been redefined. This only points out the subjective basis underneath virtually every business or management indicator and reinforces the notion that change is subjectively determined.

No further examples are necessary to demonstrate to people in the world of business that the impacts of change are subjectively felt. Simply ask those who trade in stocks, commodities, or futures. What hurts one business can help another. What helps one a lot may help others very little.

3. Change is not easily unitized.

Today's winners have quit trying to measure change with yesterday's crude tools. They realize the tenuous and often foolish nature of our attempts to isolate change. We need to see all its dimensions, even those overlooked by our competitors, who are still struggling to categorize it. Our focus is on using it, not scrutinizing it.

Civilizations unitized time by fixing its increments (day, hour, minute, second, etc.) and standardizing its measurement. Until this occurred, commercial dialogue, scientific analysis, and daily communication were riddled with subjectively. The result was an economy stunted by human limits to growth and progress, most caused by this nonuniform, unsynchronized activity.

Time continues to be subjectively experienced (2 weeks spent in prison seem much longer than 2 weeks enjoying a vacation), but it is always reducible to objective measurement (2 weeks is always 2 weeks, regardless of how they are spent and by whom).

Our concept of *value* has also been unitized and made objective, through the invention of money. Even dynamic differences in time and value have been accommodated (theories of relativity, currency indexes, currency futures, and so on). The same cannot be said for change, though. It remains the most elusive commercial variable. We don't have "change

gauges" on our wrists or "change ledgers" in our accounting depart-
ments.

4. Change is nonexistent without effects.

*We need to know what change does or doesn't do, not simply what it is.
Most important, we will want to maximize its benefits and dodge its
damage.*

Remember our definition of "change" as difference (effects) occurring
over time. Dynamic differences are the result of the mechanisms of
change operating on whatever we manage (or do not manage). Even if
we need not spend much effort justifying this notion, fully compre-
hending its meaning is important.

Seeing and Feeling Change

Change presents greater challenges than merely its identification, for
knowing it exists helps very little. We need a knowledge of its nature,
its personality, its behavior. The search for this knowledge is quite frustrating, for exploring the phenomenon of change is much like exploring
the secrets of the cosmos: the more we learn, the more we appreciate
how little we know. Perhaps "knowledge" is the wrong word; perhaps
we should be attempting to feel change, to "sense" it intuitively rather
than to "know" it through the scientific method. What makes this em-
pirical knowledge so difficult to attain is the variable and indeterminate
nature of the subject, the fact that change defies rational attempts to
understand and, especially, to manipulate it.

This is an extraordinary finding, considering that the conventional
challenge and measure of a business manager centers around the ability
to detect and manipulate changes for the better. In order to test this
wisdom further, let's consider the frustration with which change is studied.

5. Change defies cause-and-effect analysis.

*Only by appreciating the limits of our understanding can we begin to
harness the power of what we do know. Scholars are interested in the
underlying meaning and the all-encompassing law. We will tap the
pragmatic lessons and leave the deeper understanding to the researchers.*

What is called the "scientific method" has formed the basis for probing
the unknown in virtually every area of investigation. It involves the
recognition and formulation of a problem, the collection of data through

observation (sampling, testing, experiment), and the development and testing of hypotheses based on the data. Business managers, whether or not they know it, have been using the scientific method for centuries to improve their understanding of and impact on commercial enterprises. When a company, wishing to stimulate sales of a consumer product, increases advertising efforts and then measures any increase (change) in number of products sold, it has taken the three steps outlined here for the scientific method. It has:

1. Formulated the problem (increased advertising could lead to increased sales).

2. Collected observable data (the increase in advertising and the commensurate increase in sales have been quantified).

3. Developed a hypothesis based on that data (increased advertising leads to increased sales).

Of course, much more detailed observation and analysis is typically involved to answer specific questions such as these: What type of advertising has the greatest impact on sales? What is the ratio between dollars spent for each type of advertisement and ensuing sales? Is there a limit (are there diminishing returns) to the effectiveness of further increases in advertising effort? All these applications are merely extensions of the scientific method as it can be applied to certain variables in the mix that leads to more or fewer sales of the product.

The nature of the relationship between cause and effect—its clarity, consistency, and ability to be proved again and again (its repeatability)—is the prize at the end of all the testing, sampling, and observation: the fruit of the scientific method. Knowledge of and confidence in that relationship create a powerful tool in the business manager's hands. He or she can, theoretically, maximize effects beneficial to the firm (sales) while minimizing the cost required to achieved them (advertising). In other words, the relationship can be optimized.

The Challenge of Optimization

Optimization will become a key principle in our developing understanding of the effects of change. After all, what else could be the duty of business management than to strive for and achieve optimum results, the largest profit for the smallest investment, the greatest ROI, the maximum benefit for the minimum risk, the "biggest bang for the buck"?

Our ability to optimize relies on a series of known and repeatable relationships between causes and effects, usually derived from applying the scientific method to our business environment. Were we to live and operate in a world where relationships remained stable, where differences were static and not dynamic, where conditions remained consistent enough to isolate causes and tie them to effects without the disruption or interference caused by extraneous factors, the challenge of optimization would be rather straightforward.

Unfortunately, our world is quite different. It is dominated by the unpredictable, by the interplay of thousands of factors within even the most simple of relationships, and by constantly shifting environments wherein it is impossible to isolate causes and effects and match them in a convenient series of one-to-one sets.

Manager as Manipulator?

This is not to say that the scientific method and the resulting cause-and-effect relationships it attempts to uncover have no place in the real world of business and commerce. They remain the basic analytic tools we use to better understand how things tie together and what we can do to take advantage of those ties. The very essence of business effectiveness is to isolate and understand not only the simple but the complex relationships that exist in the realm of our grasp and to use that understanding to improve our position and our performance. Indeed, much of today's fascination with so-called management information systems is the presumed power they give us to solve the relationships so critical to our success. "Management ability," then, can be defined in terms of competence in recognizing relationships and manipulating them effectively.

As our appreciation of the role of change unfolds, though, we shall see just how difficult recognition and manipulation can become. Change itself is both a cause and an effect; it is more than merely one more variable demanding our attention and observation. It is indeed not a variable one can manipulate, but a force acting in spurious, unpredictable ways upon all other variables. "Who can say what the dance of variables will produce tomorrow . . . next month . . . next year? Surprise is inherent in nature" (Ferguson, 1980, p. 157).

Equations, Relationships, and Models

In order to demonstrate the ability of change to defy or frustrate cause-and-effect analysis, let's continue the example of the relationship between sales and advertising. Suppose, after numerous manipulations of advertising expenditures and subsequent observation of sales volume, we were confident that a 30 percent increase in advertising usually resulted in a 15 percent increase in sales.

Provided that the profit generated by increases in sales compensated for the extra cost of advertising, we would conclude that increased advertising was beneficial. Of course, the relationship would prove to vary once saturation was reached, or once the law of diminished returns took over, but our assumption would have been "proved" by the scientific method.

Knowing this relationship, we could use similar methods to determine the relationship between price reductions and sales volume. Let's say that, within limits, for every 10 percent reduction in price, sales would jump 20 percent.

Putting both price and advertising together (the "marketing mix"), we could now presume that tradeoffs could be made between increased advertising and decreased price, for both would have a positive impact on sales. We could combine these two relationships so that an increase in advertising expenditure of 1 percent would have the same impact on sales as a 1 percent reduction in price: powerful knowledge with which to manage the advertising, pricing, and sales of our product.

A Foundation of Shifting Sand

What is wrong with this elementary example? A number of things. First, we assumed that the independently ascertained relationships are fixed and repeatable, that they will not change as we move through time or apply them to different volumes of each. Second, we artificially fixed a great number of dependent and independent variables (other than price and advertising), which we know act upon sales. These include consumer preference; product needs, usage, and availability; buying patterns; seasonality; economic conditions; the actions or inactions of competitors; and distribution effectiveness, to name only a few.

Our crude model (in terms of the scientific method: the way we formulated the problem) was sensitive to none of these factors. All were presumed fixed—invariant, constant, unchanging. We know that no such assumptions are valid. Change impacts all these factors, and a change in any one of them causes change in others, the result of which impacts sales. The effect of changing social values (megachange) could reduce the demand for our product and counter increases in sales that would otherwise have been stimulated by advertising or price manipulation. Price cutting by competitors (macrochange) could reduce the effectiveness of our reductions. A change in the use of our product (microchange) could further impact sales and disrupt the presumed relationships we established, relationships we assumed to be oblivious to any such effects.

Suppose our product was table salt. Increased public perceptions that excess salt (sodium) is harmful to health could cause reduced sales (megachange: the trend toward higher consciousness of health and nutrition). The decreased price of a competitor's salt would have the same effect (macrochange: growing competition among salt producers). And the switch from salt to another chemical compound in the ingredient mix of a major industrial customer might likewise destroy the viability of our price-advertising-sales relationship (microchange: the discovery of a better process in the chemical industry).

The lesson is that change greatly limits both the establishment and the application of cause-and-effect relationships. Certainly these should still be pursued. Typically, however, this is feasible only in limited cases, in fairly stable environments, and for basic one-to-one relationships. *Change doesn't entirely destroy the notion of the scientific method;* change simply casts doubt upon the universal value of the scientific method and warns us of the danger we face when we rely on its results.

More Reasons for Failure

Because trust in the scientific method is so ingrained in our psyches, so well reinforced by our educational system, and because even the most open-minded managers harbor deep affection for its principles, despite the problem of change, we need to mention a few more reasons why the scientific method fails us.

1. *Cumulative effects are often ignored.* Some effects become noticeable or pronounced only after some sort of artificial or real *tolerance thresholds* are exceeded. That is to say, we may tweak a certain management variable time and time again, with no perceptible impacts (changes in other factors or results) until a certain nth change causes distinct, often massive results, even catastrophe. Until such a point is reached, we may model our mental picture of our business mix as independent of or *unresponsive* to our manipulated variable (the one we tweaked over and over again).

The worlds of science and business abound with examples. In material science, the "elastic limit" is one such threshold. Business practitioners are schooled in a similar phenomenon: *price inelasticity.* In both examples, using physical as well as price elasticity and plasticity, a point is reached at which the cumulative effects of past changes take over, with a nonlinear result. The expression "the straw that broke the camel's back" is a more succinct way of describing this principle.

2. *People confound direct analysis.* What makes people tick? What stimuli make them jump, change, and react? And how do they do so? Answering these questions is well beyond the scope intended here. Suffice it to say that people do not react as predictably as Newtonian objects, machines, or even sophisticated processes. They respond to inner drives as well as external factors, and to various interactions of the two. The problem with most management models, and most management actions aimed at change, is that the dynamic, ever-changing forces driving people are usually indeterminate or unknown, even to the individuals themselves. Although more will be said later about the uses and misuses of people, for now we must admit that people are the wild card in our business deck. They are the greatest unknown.

3. *It is generally impossible to reduce a cause to its affective essence.* The scientific method and trial and error (simulation) both attempt to isolate causes by manipulating input and observing resultant output, by squeezing one variable and listening for one or more of the others to squeal. Once an active cause has been isolated, we are often unable to detect or unconcerned with that element of it which actually produced the effect: its *affective essence.*

An example best illustrates this problem. Suppose a primitive clan of cave dwellers was at an early stage of agricultural development, trying to plant and harvest meager crops. A scientific-minded member, after throwing leftover drippings of community stew on a particular plant, discovered, through serendipity, that this particular plant grew much better than the rest. Stopping there, the lesson was that plants do better when fed stew drippings, and the entire clan commenced nightly feedings of stew drippings to each plant—reaping, we should add, higher yields as a result. From our perspective, atop the shoulders of such ancestors, we know the affective essence of the change (feeding stew drippings) was the liquid content—the water. Plants grew better when watered, not only when fed stew drippings.

As absurd as this story appears, it is surprising how primitive we still are when it comes to the isolation of affective essence among the variables we manipulate. How often do we stop at a pragmatic solution without fully uncovering the active agent or process it embodies? Even now, all over the world, well-intentioned, educated managements are still missing the essence of change—still throwing stew drippings on their crops and being elated and self-satisfied with the results. One can imagine a group of executives sitting around a cocktail table (rather than a campfire) listening to one member announcing a revolutionary stew-drippings discovery. Perhaps this member pauses and asks for more funds to explore the phenomenon even further. To which, we can be sure, a senior responds, "Hell, if it works now, who cares? Don't change it!"

4. *We often neglect the limits of causality.* This statement is closely aligned with the sentiment in statement 1 regarding tolerance thresholds. It refers to instances in which, for some reason beyond our ability to perceive, the nature of causality changes. The field of productivity analysis yields many examples. Suppose we are measuring output per worker and determine it to be 50 units per day. Extrapolation of this causality equation (1 worker = 50 units per day) leads us to conclude that by adding another worker we always achieve, more or less, 50 additional units for each day the second worker is employed. When certain unforeseen limits are reached, however, we may receive much more or much less per worker.

Suppose a physical limit (such as crowding, work interference, or congestion) is encountered at some "critical mass" of workers, say 20. Or maybe efficiencies are gained through interaction (cooperation) among workers such that, say, 1 worker holding a board while another nails it results in more than twice as many boards nailed per day than if 2 workers were each separately attempting to simultaneously hold and nail. In that case, 2 workers produce more than twice what 1 worker does ($2 > 2 \times 1$). Adding a third worker only interferes; we get less than a 50 percent increase because either (1) the new worker must go back to separate hold-nail activity, thereby becoming less productive than the 2-worker team alongside, or (2) 3 workers in a hold-nail team get in each other's way, frustrate each other, and result in net loss of productivity (if not a fistfight). As we will see later, change in this sense is seldom linear, nor is it amenable to extrapolation of results from one set of conditions to another.

5. *It is difficult to uncouple symbiotic causes and effects.* The simplest way to grasp this concept is to admit that some effects lead to others; that some effects, in essence, become causes themselves. Causes and effects often feed each other, and given certain conditions, chain reactions develop, the extent of which we are unable to predict or even trace once they occur.

Imagine a quiet room filled to capacity with contented house cats. Into this tranquil setting we could toss a powerful firecracker (a cause), with chaotic results. After several minutes, once all the screeching, jumping, spitting, biting, and clawing had subsided, how could anyone (or any computer model) reconstruct events to determine whether a particular scratch on a certain cat was attributable to the original blast (the first cause), the first startled jump of a cat (one effect), the ensuing inadvertent bite of a third (another cause and effect), or something else? Even the cats themselves wouldn't know.

Or imagine a convoluted chain-reaction automobile mishap on a busy expressway during rush hour, where 75 cars are involved, each damaged. At whom does the owner of the forty-third car point for culpability, for causing the damage to that particular vehicle? All the world's scientists, physicians, and attorneys (who would no doubt also become involved) couldn't untangle distinct cause-and-effect relationships here. The resulting chaos would be similar in significance, and appearence, to our roomful of terror-stricken cats.

The inability to tie cause to effect in a simple one-to-one relationship has led to more educated awe than confidence about changes in the world around us. It has prompted strong criticism of classical scientific analysis, especially from such futurists as Jeremy Rifkin, who writes

> The idea that specific phenomena can be isolated from the rest of the universe they're a part of and then connected in some kind of "pure" causal relationships with other isolated phenomena is just plain wrong thinking. . . .
> Everything in this world is connected with everything else in a delicate and complex web of interrelationships. The best computer ever designed by humankind cannot calculate even a tiny fraction of all the relationships that exist in the ecosystem of a simple pond. Scientists have tried it and have only thrown up their hands in despair after realizing the complexity and detail involved (Rifkin & Howard, 1980, p. 223).

In *The Aquarian Conspiracy* Marilyn Ferguson describes the emergent general systems theory: "each variable in any system interacts with the other variables so thoroughly that cause and effect cannot be separated. A single variable can be cause and effect. Reality will not be stilled. And it cannot be taken apart" (1980, p. 157).

6. *We cannot quantify the value of timing.* A successful business effort or manager is often seen as the product of good timing. "Timing" refers to that magic moment when conditions are just right for the introduction and maximum effect of a specific cause. The same cause could be activated either before or after that ripe time to no avail, except utter failure. Granted that "Timing is everything," as the saying goes, how do we tie cause to effect without considering timing? We obviously can't, and yet neither can we define or quantify the value of timing itself. Timing plays an important role in many efforts, but it cannot be counted upon, planned, or quantified.

7. *Our observation interferes with the phenomena being observed.* Market surveys, productivity analyses, work sampling, and even medical

and scientific experiments seeking to tie cause to effect suffer from this principle. It renders all but the most carefully designed studies suspect.

Consumers asked to express a preference for one "blind" product over another typically want to help, to come to a conclusion. Those who detest both choices usually pick one or the other. Those preferring a nonoffered alternative do not mention it, or the sample mechanism has no provision for recording it. Doctors experimenting with medications have seen similar effects: improvement in the group given no effective medication whatsoever—the "placebo effect." And even nuclear physicists cannot peer directly at subatomic particles because the light needed to "see" them changes them.

The most familiar business example of the interference of observation with change is the Hawthorne experiments, in which the measured effects of workplace changes in a manufacturing plant were muted or amplified by the subjects' (workers') knowledge or suspicion that they were being studied. Observation changes the observed.

8. *We minimize the burden of simulation.* When analysts in any field of inquiry are limited by the problem of indeterminacy, they turn to simulation. Simulation requires the processing of change over hundreds or thousands of repetitions, usually with the help of computer programs, to see what happens and with what frequency. It's little more than an advanced, accelerated version of trial and error, sometimes referred to as "what if?" modeling.

The problems with applying simulation theory to real-life business decisions can be summarized as involving (a) the difficulty of creating the program (b) the impossibility of considering all interactive factors, and most important, (c) the burden of data input that is so commonly overlooked by those who design and install computer-based information systems. In many cases, by the time these problems have been overcome, the environment which the model has been created to simulate has changed to such an extent that the original program design is no longer representative of reality. It becomes a shadow of the past, and we become lost in that shadow.

The point of this argument is not to show that there is no place for rational analysis, careful observation, or investigation of the effects of change, but merely to illustrate how change, as a phenomenon rather than simply another management variable, defies our attempts to simplify and exploit our business environments. The challenge of change is *first* to understand and *then* to exploit. It's a challenge that only a select few will meet.

6. Change is not reversible.

It's senseless to try to undo change or hope that the pendulum will eventually swing back to where we are. Let's not change change, but make our ride along its journey an intelligent and profitable one.

The Newtonian principle of process reversibility holds that any process can be not only *repeated* (with the same results) but *reversed*, provided all other factors are held constant. Reversibility is a very useful as well as intrinsically beautiful principle. It allows us, in effect, to "undo" change. It is used throughout the world in chemical processes, engineering design, and mathematical reasoning, to name a few applications. It cannot, however, be applied to businesses because change cannot be so easily reversed in our operating arena.

Let's return to the basic relationships we determined for the sale of salt. Assuming that all other factors could be held constant (although we know they can't) and that our advertising-price-sales relationships have proved valid and repeatable, can we reverse their results? Let's suppose we decide that we have decreased price too much, that for some reason we would like to increase price by 11.1 percent (back to the original level after one reduction of 10 percent). Can we assume to reverse the change in sales according to our formula (a decrease in price results in twice the commensurate increase in sales)? According to Newtonian mechanics we can. But even our natural intuition, without any evidence, tells us this is probably not so; and experimentation would most likely substantiate our doubts. Why is this?

Can We Undo Change?

To begin with, people are not Newtonian objects, not simply billiard balls waiting to be pushed one way or the other. Whereas all billiard balls may be assumed to be identical, not all salt consumers are identical. Each of our customers did not increase his or her consumption by exactly 20 percent after the original price decrease. Some may have increased their purchases of salt by 30 percent or even higher. Some may have actually decreased their purchases. All we know is that the *aggregate effect* of all their individual purchases was 20 percent higher. We know nothing about individual changes.

In addition, billiard balls have no memory. They simply react to the application of each force as if it were the first and only one. They do not remember the first impact (or force) and modify their behavior before or during the second application of force based on that past experience. Were our ball a person, however, he or she would realize the impending second force was coming; would wince, dodge, or lean one way or another; and would thereby interfere with the action and change the resulting effect.

Consumers also remember. They don't forget the initial reduction in the price of salt, rebounding back to their original buying habits once the counteracting (reversed) price increase returns their cost to its initial level. *They have changed* because of the original process. They are different, they view our product differently, they value it differently, they will never see it the same again, regardless of our attempts to recreate the past.

Our original pricing change had a measurable impact on their aggregate buying activity, and it also had countless unknown, immeasurable secondary impacts on their perceptions, needs, product uses, and knowledge of or exposure to competitors' products or substitutes. We focused our attention on the directly manipulable variables (price and advertising), but this does not mean we fixed the thousands of others. We simply ignored them. This is why we cannot reverse their effects by simply reversing our figurative force. We cannot undo consumer impressions, perceptions, or values, nor can we erase the experience (and it subjective impacts) from their memories. We cannot reverse the process—cannot undo change.

7. Change can dilate, contract, and float.
By understanding these complexities we will know when to try to control events and when to accept them. We'll also know more about the value of our management tools and how to keep them from making fools of us.

Because change, like time, is essentially an anthropocentric concept and because it is subjectively determined and its impacts are subjectively felt, change shares with time the ability to dilate, contract, and float. By "dilation" we mean the real or seeming ability to expand, to stretch, or to assume a greater dimension given certain relativistic conditions. The opposite of "dilation" is "contraction," the compression or shrinking of change. "Float" relates to time lags inherent in the activity of change and attributed to the time needed between the actual initiation of change and our eventual discernment of its results. By understanding the concepts of change dilation, contraction, and float, you become better able to control it or at least accommodate it to your advantage.

Dilation and Contraction

Change dilation occurs when the effect of a cause of change is latent, simmering, or inactive until it either gradually or suddenly appears much later. Sometimes this involves the festering or growth of effects (or their compounding with others) until positive or negative signals appear on management reports, financial statements, or sales analyses. We might assume in those cases that change took a long time to occur (dilated), but it may be that the cause was immediate, with only the effects late in appearing.

Change compression involves a shortening of this cause-and-effect span, and in certain instances, effects we would expect to attribute to a cause actually appear *before* the cause itself (negative time lag). Most often this happens when the knowledge of impending change precedes its occurrence and conditions react in anticipation of the forthcoming change. This phenomenon is particular to changes employing or applied upon people, for people can and do sense impending change rather adroitly. Billiard balls and other figurative objects can't anticipate forces about to arrive; people certainly can.

Consumers react to suspected or announced changes as well, some accelerating purchase decisions, some delaying them—for example, when a newer model, upgraded version, or technological breakthrough is anticipated. The expectation of change can have dramatic and unpredictable results in business, results sometimes eclipsing those brought about by the actual change itself. Astute businesses often reap huge rewards by using the power of *change anticipation*.

Float

When we speak of "float" in relation to change, we use the term very loosely. "Change float" is the time elapsing between initiation of change (cause) and perception of (feeling or seeing) its impacts. It can be divided into two elements: (1) the lag between the cause of change and its effects and (2) the subsequent lag between the occurrence of an effect and our perception of it. Change float abounds in our society as a whole and in our business activities in particular. In terms of variable manipulation (management-originated change, such as our reduction in the price of salt), change float is the time between our squeezing of one variable and our hearing the screams of other affected variables.

As we shall discover when addressing business reactions to change, float is a critical feature of the change phenomenon. Most of our management information systems (be they crude observation or highly mechanized procedures) foster change float. Lags abound, especially with advanced telemetry systems (management reporting) and for managers who are spatially and conceptually removed from that which they "manage." Of course, this lack of management proximity generally leads to use of cumbersome managerial scaffolding as a substitution, and float thrives in the cracks and gaps of that scaffolding.

Change Malleability

We can summarize the malleable nature of change by suggesting that it may affect the value of many other managerial tools presently in use, particularly business models and management reporting systems. Here are some ways this occurs:

1. As change data are transformed in the information pipeline, knowledge or appreciation of the change is reduced: *line loss.*

2. Summarization of change data (up the chain of command) homogenizes the distinct character of each change: *flattening change.*

3. Change reporting generally focuses on effects, not causes or their correction: *history, not control.*

4. Insensitive management models (or mindsets) lead to change dilation: *information shock.*

5. Supersensitive management models lead to change contraction: *change fakes us out.*

8. Change is a variable.

To profit from change we need to keep constantly alert to its variable nature. We'll dispel common myths that are giving its victims a false sense of security and frustrating people who can't enjoy it.

Some of the most foolish business decisions, having the most disastrous consequences, are based on the presumption that change is constant, either in its absolute value or in its rate. Intelligent observers have long held that "the only thing constant about business activity is change," but many have failed to recognize that change itself is never constant in its direction, pace, path, or rate of change (acceleration or deceleration). The most advanced understanding of change includes an appreciation of its variable and volatile nature.

Far from being merely an agent acting upon other variables in the practice of management, change is the most indeterminate variable of them all. Many highly successful businesses owe their position to an ability to outguess the movement of change. Conversely, the road to success is strewn with the carcasses of those who considered change a constant.

The Nostalgia of Fixed Constants

Each of us has been exposed to people who, lamenting the complexity of today's business world, yearn for the much simpler days of the past. To them, the past is a time when business conditions were fairly stationary and predictable, when company objectives were simple and few, when the span between management causes and their subsequent effects was narrow and direct. Climbing the corporate ladder depended on one's ability to learn lessons that lay fixed for the learning, and to apply them to similar conditions with fairly predictable results. Of course, it was never all that simple, and hard work, luck, and timing were needed, but the point is that rational lessons and management approaches one developed during business apprenticeship could be translated into effective guides and techniques for the future.

How things have changed! For today and the foreseeable future we know that business conditions are anything but stationary, company objectives are complex and situational (if enunciated at all), the span between cause and effect is wide, and the connection often defies analysis. And not only is it difficult to coalesce meaningful lessons during the dynamic years of one's education and apprenticeship, but any lessons thus learned may become obsolete by the time one is in a position to apply them. According to Ferguson, "Our ideas about work, money, and management grew out of an old stable social order irrelevant to present flux" (1980, p. 326).

Listen to a middle-level manager describing ITT after deregulation: "Dealing with unpredictability is something the industry is not used to. The top managers are good men, smart men, but they wish the world was once again predictable and stable" (Green & Berry, 1985, p. 57). We know that it won't be, and because it won't, our managers will have to abandon the nostalgia of fixed constants and focus on flux instead.

When we consider the concept of change as the ultimate variable and relate contemporary business conditions to the past, it is no wonder that the "nostalgia of fixed constants" has so much allure. Coming to grips with change as a persistent and varying factor in our lives and our business efforts requires an understanding of the differences between yesterday and today, and the realization that they are attributable to the variable nature of change. Put simply, *change changes*. To illustrate the ways in which this simple fact has been overlooked, we should examine both *what change is not* and some mistakes based on the presumption that some aspects of change are constant.

The Extrapolation Trap

The first concerns the nonlinear nature of change, its failure to move at a constant pace or in a constant direction. If we plot change effects (number of cars per household, average family income, etc.) against elapsed time, we err when we presume that what went on in the past can be extrapolated into the future (i.e., that we can extend the line from today into tomorrow or the next decade). This means that linear trends and linear extrapolation based thereon are fallacious and dangerous.

Countless examples exist. One involves projection of demand for electricity, whereby rates of demand increase (5 to 6 percent per year) experienced in the 1950s and 1960s were expected to continue in the 1970s and 1980s (when 0 to 2 percent per year growth was actually experienced in many areas). Those making these naive projections (linear extrapolations in most cases) suffered from the allure of the nostalgia of fixed constants. They assumed other variables in the demand mix—such as (1) price elasticity; (2) effect of conservation measures; (3) economic activity; (4) viability of alternate sources (gas, oil, solar, biomass); and (5) family, community, and national demographic patterns—to be fixed. We know now that they weren't fixed.

Why We Do Not Live On Pluto

That attempts to project change linearly into the future (or even exponentially, as when one assumes change will accelerate at a constant rate) can become quite ludicrous is demonstrated by some of the most outrageous projections about life today made by futurists of the past. According to many of them, we should now be living on other planets, perhaps commuting by spaceship to an atomic factory where robotic housekeepers or self-mowing lawns are manufactured. So much for linear extrapolation. As Toffler warns us, when looking into the future, "we must resist the temptation to be seduced by straight lines" (1980, p. 124).

No Simple Harmonic Motion

Other misconceptions include the assumptions that change is consistent in effect and that it is periodic or harmonic in nature, like a swinging pendulum (what goes around comes around). Neither is true. First, let's dispense with consistency in effect. The same change made under two different sets of conditions can result in dramatically different reactions. This is true whether change occurs in different cultures or locations, under different economic situations, or at different times. The concepts discussed above—such as irreversibility, dilation, contraction, float, and timing—substantiate the inconsistent nature of change.

To describe change as acting like a pendulum swinging back and forth is to neglect several fundamental aspects of life. First, simply because trends or fashions appear to fluctuate, say from liberal to conservative and back again, doesn't mean they return to their precise previous conditions. Change may double back on itself, to be sure, returning to some aspects of the past, but these are incomplete, different, and modified by experience that developed between the past and the present. Even the principle of irreversibility destroys the notion of harmonic changes. Surely those who sense periodic motion in change realize that the pendulum never fully returns to its previously held position, but simply shifts to a previously taken path, leading to a new, never-before-realized destination.

There's no simple analog, no basic "scientific program" underlying change that merits the time and effort needed to pursue it. At some point we must stop trying to *simplify* change and start to *use* it.

Technology's Passenger?

We can hope that the events of this decade, if not the past century, have finally shattered a common perception of change: that it occurs only along a technological axis and in lockstep with advances in technology. This was the major mistake made by futurists of the past who would have had us by now eating "encapsulated space nutrients" for dinner instead of sushi. They saw changing technology as the bow of a ship plying time, with other, minor changes (spinoffs) following in its wake. Unfortunately, there are many today who still worship technology as the arrow of change, constantly flying upward. Even those who recognize the problems and penalties of advancing technology (pollution, resource depletion, human alienation) often see social or economic changes only along the technological axis.

Of all the misconceptions regarding change, this is perhaps the most commonly held. The relationship can be expressed this way:

Technology = change = progress

Most technologists will admit that life isn't so simple. They know that technological changes are often caused by serendipity, that there is no telling how a breakthrough will impact our lives, or when or why.

Technology doesn't necessarily lead to progress, nor does it spearhead the parade of change. Other happenings in other realms—social, political, natural, psychological, spiritual, cultural, and environmental, to name a few—can have more dramatic, more pervasive effects. Change occurs in all arenas, not just the technical.

Nor does technology meet the ever-increasing human needs often intensified by change. According to Naisbitt, "In our minds, at least, technology is always on the verge of liberating us from personal discipline and responsibility. Only it never does and it never will" (1982, p. 53).

A Drunk in a Dark Alley

But if change doesn't proceed along a fixed axis (such as the technical one), doesn't travel in a periodic orbit, doesn't move at a constant or constantly varying speed, how does it proceed? The answer can be given in two ways: by a logical, carefully crafted expression or by simile. First the logical expression:

Change occurs nonuniformly and inconsistently, the result of an indeterminate array of interactive, irreversible cause-and-effect relationships acting with unknown intermediate and final results.

Now the simile:

Change is like a drunk in a dark alley. It lurches, staggers, weaves, stops, and jumps at ghosts, all the time striking and bouncing off whatever is nearby.

Of the two, the second description is easier to remember and closer to the truth.

9. Our ability to see change is limited by us.
What we don't know and what we don't foresee will hurt us. *We control how much we do of both. Change control begins with removal of our perception barriers. We create them, we can dismantle them.*

The premise of this and the next principle is that, except in rare cases, business managers do not manage reality but do manage models or contrived representations of reality.

A feature distinguishing humans from other animals is our ability to conceive and manipulate symbols, abstractions, and representations. Whether we realize it or not, our thoughts, plans, and stores of knowledge all involve figurative and literal models of reality as we know it.

We constantly construct, modify, and enhance these models in order to more closely align them with perceived reality and to make them more effective and reliable tools for understanding and predicting events in our lives. Models that prove to be out of synchronization with our experience are renovated or demolished, and newer, "more accurate" ones are adopted. This constant modification of our mental pictures of life keeps us current, effective, and "adjusted."

Playing with Models

We constantly create not only mental but physical models of our business conditions, using them to understand what is going on in reality and to test (simulate) management actions upon reality. Why discuss models here? In their most general sense, models represent the way we look at and operate in our changing world. Examples of business models range from the basic, such as budgets, schedules, reports, organization charts, position descriptions, procedures, designs, surveys, and studies, to fairly sophisticated ones including strategic plans, on-line inventories, interactive simulation programs, decision trees, delphi broadcasting, material management systems, and job function analyses.

Whether crude or exotic, primitive or technologically advanced, manual or automated, belonging solely in one person's mind or owned and operated by scores of managers in unison, each model is limited, contrived, and of no intrinsic value. Its only value is derived from the benefits it brings its users. Business models are tools, not ends in themselves, and the nature of change is that it mocks most of them.

Reality: The Most Accurate Model

If we were able to construct a wholly complete, detailed, and perfectly representative model, we would not have a model at all, but a recreation of reality. This is not only impossible but foolish to attempt, for the value of models is their ability to simplify reality—making it easier to understand and to manipulate. Simplification involves shortcuts, facades, analogy, and the search for bare essentials (the affective essence of our setting) unencumbered by constants, inactive variables, and extraneous components which cloud our view and distort our actions. The search for a perfect model, then, does not result in the most complex or "realistic" version but the most pragmatic one: the one that balances simplicity with accuracy, cost with benefit.

Every management model, of whatever type and cost, should be sensitive to change. Since we are the architects and builders of all models, we alone determine this sensitivity; we alone design and operate our models in a way that accommodates or ignores the phenomenon of change to one degree or another. Because even the most sophisticated of models is merely a crude shadow of reality (and rightfully so), our ability to understand and respond to the phenomenon of change (to see it, to manage in it) is limited by the way we build and use our models— limited by us.

The Price of Sensitivity

Suppose reality is an electric generating station under construction. If we want to monitor productivity by geographic area (within the plant site), construction craft, contractor and subcontractor, and type of work, we will need a gigantic model, for each of these dimensions can comprise from 1 to 100 categories.

Suppose there are 10 areas within the plant boundary, 21 craft categories, 6 contractors, 15 subcontractors under each contractor, and 8 general work operations (such as lift, support, align, apply, inspect) for each craft. The total potential model elements are $10 \times 21 \times 6 \times 15 \times 8$, or 151,200! System costs, data input, and management analysis of results would be staggering.

An alternative of reporting by contractor and area only (6×10) would leave 60 categories of data, a much more reasonable, though cruder and less "realistic," model. When deciding between these two options (or others), management should weigh the value (managerial significance) of the information each model provides against the cost and secondary penalties each exacts.

The Escape of Information

Suppose we chose the second option, and we were planning and monitoring work by contractor and geographic area. Further assume that one craft category (let's say ironworkers) is behind schedule, inefficient, and causing a tremendous amount of rejected work. Since our cruder model doesn't capture performance data by craft classification (comparing such to planned schedules, standard production and rejection rates, etc.) we would not see this change directly. Our reporting system would be insensitive to it, giving us only masked, secondary "indicators" that something might be going wrong with certain contractors and in certain areas (probably those involving ironworkers).

We would have to interpret, extrapolate, speculate, or investigate further. The model would be set aside or deemed useless for this needed analysis. Ideally, we would eventually trace the problem to its source (ironworkers), but had other crafts (say, masons or pipefitters) performed better than planned, their positive work variances could have countered (and thereby eliminated from our view) the negative performance of the ironworkers—giving us no reason to investigate outside the realm of the model because the model would tell us, in aggregate, that all was well. Change has a way of hiding in models.

More Model Problems

Models are contrived by people; and the models we create have obvious inadequacies caused by our pragmatism and our willingness to create and operate them in view of their respective costs. Models also have other problems.

1. *Models are costly and time-consuming to build.* Often two negative results ensue: (*a*) the model becomes an object of infatuation (it's fun to create and play with). This diverts management attention from its ultimate goal—reality. Also, (*b*) reality proceeds faster or in different directions from the development of the model, leading to lags or lack of synchronization between the two.

2. *Models are fixed.* Most models are static—not moving or changing. Reality, as we know, is dynamic. When reality presents changing risks, information needs, or management objectives, fixed models can't adapt—can't "pivot." Listen to Rifkin: "The old Newtonian view that treats all phenomena as isolated components of matter, or fixed stocks, has given way to the idea that everything is part of a dynamic flow." (Rifkin & Howard, 1980, p. 223).

3. *Models point in a few directions.* Models represent only certain anticipated aspects of reality. Whenever other aspects demand attention (our business complexion changes) models can become obsolete. Reality changes along hundreds of axes, while models are typically aligned only along a few.

4. *Models create change distortions and float.* Time lags, insensitivity below design thresholds, and the transposition of data from one stage in the information pipeline to another amplify the propensity of change to dilate, contract, and float. If we think of reality as a distant star and

remember that each star is light-years away, we realize that when we gaze "at the star" we are not seeing present reality (the star), but an image of a star as it existed years ago. That image has been distorted and filtered by its passage through space and time, and shaped by the capacity of our telescope.

All these considerations apply to the vast majority of today's management models and the way each of us looks at our changing world. What we see at the receiving end of the pipeline is old and distorted, and is filtered and selected by our model and our use of it. Again, what we see is limited by us; we decide how much to invest in the detection of change. This is one of the most significant decisions an executive can make.

Before leaving the subject of management via models we must mention one more reason why they fail to detect changes clearly: the limited capacity of management focus. As Naisbitt suggests, "A person can only keep so many problems and concerns in his or her head or heart at any one time. If new problems or concerns are introduced, some existing ones are given up" (1982, p. 4). Business managers are no different. When given a complex report they tend to focus on four or five key elements, or important indicators (in their individual views), and see how they are doing. Change, however, is not so self-restricted. It can strike and affect many variables and show up in many areas of any report (or none at all).

Measuring but Not Feeling

Another factor in change is the inability of most common business tools to deal with nonquantifiable information—things that aren't easily reduced to or represented by numbers. "In our lives and in our cultural institutions we have been poking at qualities with tools designed to detect quantities" (Ferguson, 1980, p. 176).

In dealing with qualitative variables we tend to force them into quantitative clothing (such as percentage of customers expressing a strong dislike for our product, or number of respondents "highly excited" by our advertising campaign). Quantification of qualitative information is in itself a filter, albeit an often unavoidable one. We find it difficult to arrange, tabulate, and summarize impressions, "excitement," "dislike," or other feelings. We *measure* feelings sometimes, but we do not *feel* them through our models. Something is lost.

Finally, we must recognize that most business tools assume that those variables which cannot be manipulated are fixed, or in other words, they ignore these "fixed variables." Ignored variables are the secret hiding places of change. Like a fungus, change sometimes grows faster and more virulently when unnoticed and undisturbed—in the dark. And if we can't see change, we have little chance of accommodating or exploiting it.

10. Our ability to manage in change is limited by our ability to see change.
Today's popular management aids mask or distort the nature of change and deceive us about its impacts. With an expanded change perception we gain an expanded and often unique power to improve. Considering the future, this is the ultimate competitive edge.

We can't manage what we don't see, and we can't see what our models can't show us. This is why model selection and basic business viewpoints are so important to managing in change. This simple principle is often ignored. Here's why.

1. The people who "see" change are not always the ones who act on it. Summarization of change information leads to its dilution, both up and down hierarchical channels.

2. When we observe for the purpose of optimizing process outcomes, we focus so closely on affected variables (fuel consumption, temperature, sales of one type, warranty repairs of another type, etc.) that we tend to shut out other, perhaps changing, variables.

3. Because most of us specialize rather than generalize in our education and business apprenticeship, we develop a somewhat fixed focus of investigation along a fixed axis. That is, we tend to look only at certain areas of interest or concern and to look at these as closely as we can. We miss seeing the forest because we are leaf experts. Although we tend to see changes in our specialty area quite well, we often miss those that are spread across many areas.

4. We all suffer from information overload, and when our tolerance thresholds are exceeded we tend to shut out information, cut down the number of variables we pay attention to, and "see" only a few at a time. In other words, and in a fitting corollary to this change principle, we succumb to the approach "If we can't manage it, we don't see it."

The Reward of Understanding

The challenge of change, then, is heightened by the characteristics of the phenomenon itself and by our limited ability to discern and respond to them. But as managers, our charter is to perceive and respond to business conditions, and change is an inextricable though deceptive element of every business enterprise.

To summarize this exploration of change as a phenomenon important in all business efforts, our ability to manage is closely tied to our ability to recognize and deal with every aspect of change. We have seen and illustrated, at least in a conceptual sense applicable to most business efforts, how difficult, demanding, and *dangerous* this limitation can be. Now our attention must turn away from "what change is" to a more specific treatment of "what change means." The reward of a deeper, more intimate understanding of change is the opportunity to put that understanding to work; to use our knowledge of the characteristics of change and our appreciation of its multifaceted nature in order to meet our business objectives in a changing world; to transform the prophecy of change into our profit.

2
Breaking Free from Your Tools

Starting lean and staying agile

*I also have in mind that seemingly wealthy,
but most terribly impoverished class of all,
who have accumulated dross, but know not
how to use it, or get rid of it, and thus have
forged their own golden or silver fetters.*
HENRY DAVID THOREAU

*We need always contain within ourselves the
possibility of change; we need never be the
prisoner of yesterday's choices.*
NATHANIEL BRANDEN

No company can shift and lean with the forces of businesschange if it's
loaded down with extensive commitments and chained to fixed, demanding processes; nor can it tolerate for long any tools that *drive* the
company rather than *serve* it. The first imperative for those wishing to
survive a future of change is to shed the burden of capital—to *start
lean*—and to keep their options open as long as possible—to *stay agile*.
If we look around at companies that seem to be heeding this advice we
will probably see some or all of the following signposts of change, each

of which give noticeable evidence that the responses to change described in this chapter are being planned or carried out today.

Signposts of Change

- **More leasing and renting; less owning.** Unless a property pays for itself quickly, it will more often than not be owned only by those who lease it to others. The federal government is even considering selling Grand Coulee dam, the Postal Service, and the Federal Prison System. The British government recently sold Jaguar cars and the nation's telephone company. They call this move "privatization," but we recognize it for what it is: capital shedding. If we don't want to invest much in products, we make them disposable. If we don't want to invest much in ownership, we lease.

- **More joint ventures and other forms of risk sharing.** No one company wants to shoulder all the risks, particularly for megaprojects. A good way to mitigate risk is to spread it around. Look at how many utilities own "pieces" of nuclear power plants.

- **Fewer long-term capital expansion programs.** Capital expansion horizons are shortening because the price of long-term commitment is just too high. There may still be a lot of *plans*, but there are fewer *programs*. Plans are relatively cheap dreams. Programs take commitment. Think of the ham-and-eggs breakfast: the chicken is *involved*, but the pig is *committed*.

- **More acquisition and less creation of capital.** It is simply much safer to buy what does exist for a set price than to buy what *might* be brought about some time, in some shape, at some price. Those companies which have been burned by design and construction projects prefer a pig they can see rather than a pig in a poke.

- **Smaller product inventories.** Why speculate and float the cost of large inventory? Economies of scale aren't realized if the products aren't sold. Large inventories presume continuous, fixed demand. Change works against the stockpile.

- **More manufacturing to order (less speculation).** Computers are helping here—allowing more "tailored," on-order production runs. The shift will be from batch production to order-driven manufacturing, just as the past has shown a switch in information processing from batch to on-line modes. The future requires more programmable, flexible production runs.

- **Accelerated hardware writeoffs, shorter payback periods.** Except in basic services (electricity generation, water treatment, etc.) the rule is: If it doesn't pay itself off in a few years, it never will.

- **More demanding feasibility criteria.** As investment decisions grow in weight and importance because of change, they will be made more deliberately and with more caution. The funding hurdle for any new expenditures will be set very high.

- **Fewer megaprojects.** It will be a long time before we see the likes of new nuclear power plants, urban metros, grass-roots oil refineries, or redirected rivers. Except in cases of national emergency or national pride, forget multibillion dollar projects. To remain feasible, such projects demand that the world stand still until they are completed. It doesn't, and it won't.

- **More frequent outsourcing (buying rather than making).** Outsourcing is like leasing; it allows us to turn capacity on and off like a faucet. Yes, it costs more over the long run, but we never have the faucet open that long.

How We Became Slaves to the "Big Machine"

If there is any enduring lesson to be learned from the industrial revolution, it concerns the value of productive capital. The more a process grew in scope and capacity, the more capital we invested in it, the greater our economic benefit. Bigger machines, more comprehensive process and control systems, larger organizations, more heavily structured and fixed methods reduced the unit cost of whatever it was we produced, whether automobiles, pharmaceuticals, paper plates, or college graduates. Bigger was better. Economies of scale favored the large, stable, steady state process. According to Toffler, narrow assumptions about the nature of efficiency led modern societies to what he calls the "macrophilia of industrialism," which went hand in hand with "standardization, specialization, and the other industrial ground rules" (1980, p. 56).

Following these ground rules we created larger and larger factories, operated by larger and larger staffs, producing more and more of similar items or services. Each was optimized over time, fine-tuned, streamlined, and specialized, leading to greater returns for lesser resources. As long as most affected variables remained constant, volume was king. The enemy of the highly capitalized endeavor, though, was and remains *change*. Change throws sand into the gears of capital investment.

By "capital investment" we mean large, fixed, stationary tools, organizations, processes, and techniques—ones requiring careful planning and extensive resources before they are usable, and much "construction" time, talent, and money before the switch is pulled and benefits start tumbling out.

"Capital investment" is a term usually applied to "hard" facilities or equipment, such as machines, factories, or physical plant. We shall use the term to apply not only to hard items but to items we might call "soft," to things which, though not physical or mechanical in nature, still require costly investments and their own type of construction before they can be profitably employed. In this category we place highly stratified organizations; thorough, prescriptive "rote" procedures; and sophisticated, detailed management information systems, to name a few examples. Both hard and soft capital investments work well when carefully conceived and created under fixed conditions. Both crumble under the impact of shifting conditions, under the ripples of change.

The Burden of Capital

Larger and more extensive productive and management tools, or apparatus, are effective when we can fix many variables and exploit, in a massive way, those responding to our intervention. If we are producing automobiles, for example, we can gather all assembly functions within one huge plant; align the output of one process with the input of downstream processes; use and reuse the same productive equipment and tools over and over again; and maximize the value of fixed properties such as dies, casting equipment, lathes, cranes, and robotic welding machines. Each of these properties is extremely expensive to design and build, but once they are in place, these fixed costs are amortized over thousands or millions of units produced. The continued, consistent, and numerous uses of each make the initial investment viable. The key words here are "continued," "consistent," and "numerous." These concepts represent the foundation of the investment premise. When that foundation begins to shake, the wisdom of the investment begins to self-destruct.

Change turns the benefit of capital investment into a burden, concerning not just the high initial cost but also the restrictions a highly capitalized enterprise feels regarding its ability to shift, move, and flex to changed conditions. Massive, intricate investments are difficult to change, making adaptation to new market demands, resource mixes, and process innovations sometimes impossible without scrapping the entire investment. This is something most managements are loath to do, especially when the investment is great. We are tempted to ride out the change without adaptation or to ignore it entirely, because to respond adequately means to tamper with the great machine we have spent so much to create. With each missed opportunity to respond to change, what began as a highly efficient engine of prosperity eventually becomes a millstone around our necks, shackling us to the past.

The Costs of Capitalization

The first, direct costs of any massive capital investment (hard or soft) are usually fairly well defined and accepted. We balance these against the forecast benefits in terms of production and profit, and decide whether to invest or not. This initial feasibility hurdle is fairly straightforward, involves consideration of probability as well as presumed fixity, and once made can be tabled. We then proceed with its implementation, confident that our expectations will outweigh the initial cost. What we often fail to recognize is the hidden cost of capitalization, the price it extracts in areas not measured during the feasibility analyses.

It's important to recognize the hidden penalties of increased investment in capital, for they go way beyond the obvious costs of money, time, and developmental talents. Chief among them are the restrictions capitalization imposes on our productive and managerial flexibility. A fair presumption in this regard is that the more massive, intricate, and expensive our investment, the less likely we are to change it, or the more expensive change will be should we decide to make it. Capitalization ties us down.

Capital investments are vulnerable because they require so much. They require time, resources, management decisions, long-term commitments, and predictable uses. In an atmosphere of change, all these commodities are scarce. The presumptions of capitalization are frequently just too great, too demanding. Any capital investment presumes that the affective variables in the venture can be locked in, nailed down, or held to predictable, acceptable levels of deviation. These variables typically include prices, resource availability, competitors' actions, demand, and in the case of sophisticated management apparatus (soft property), the requisite understanding and skills needed to operate it. To the extent that all these can be stabilized during the payback period, the investment is sound. In periods of uncertainty, however, investment dependent on fixity is unsound and often difficult to obtain.

Change as a phenomenon thwarts not only general investment in ideas, apparatus, or facilities but specific investment as well. When technology is moving at a rapid pace it's difficult to convince someone to invest in what's available now. In a short time that could become obsolete, nonfeasible, a wasted investment. Political unrest and other destabilizing factors have long been known to thwart capital investment in specific areas.

Investment Requires Irrevocable Choices

A factor reducing our willingness to invest in any singular idea or facility is that saying "yes" to it means saying "no" to other choices. It requires an irrevocable choice, a strong commitment. In times of change commitments are hard to make. Not only must we say "no" to alternatives available at the time we decide upon a specific investment, but also we must give up the option of saying "yes" to those that come along in the future. Today's investment requires saying "no" to alternatives that have yet to develop, to tomorrow's opportunities. It reduces the liquidity of our assets, consuming our potential for future decisions.

Other Penalties

There are other, less obvious penalties attached to any major investment during times ripe for or undergoing change. Because capitalization involves complex, efficient apparatus, it requires long, continuous payback periods. Our hard or soft investment must be used, no matter how inappropriate or inefficient it becomes, as long as its use helps, even only partially, to defray its first cost. We end up using something that is less and less helpful and more and more burdensome. It funnels massive resources in one direction, thereby shutting off numerous potentials in other directions.

Capitalization makes us dependent, in a very serious way, upon those variables we presumed fixed. It also requires a fixing or freezing of methods, designs, or systems as they existed at the time the commitment was made, creating situations in which these become less than optimum or even obsolete during the time span between authorization of the commitment and completion of the investment. The greater the investment, the more complex and time-consuming, the more susceptible it is to the possibility of becoming obsolete before it *becomes*, before it "exists."

This phenomenon is very common with capital-intensive industrial projects, especially high-technology ventures. Rather than freeze the original design parameters, many companies attempt to catch up to moving technology as the plant is under construction. This leads to numerous, rippling changes in design, construction, and operations, each leading to more and more changes in the finished project. Companies must decide, under these circumstances, whether to pay the high price of revisions on the run or to freeze their expectations to less than state of the art in the industry. Were the initial investment simple or minor, this difficult decision would be avoided.

Management Impacts

We pay for capital investments not only with dollars and days. We pay in the way they shape our view of management functions and the way we organize, perform, and evaluate management tasks. To begin with, large investments require large, tiered organization structures to coordinate their construction and to operate them once constructed. Capital investment breeds centralization: centralized activity, centralized organizations, and centralized decision making. All these run counter to the decentralizing, diffusing forces of change.

Large organizations, singularity of purpose, massive investment in the tools people use (as opposed to the people themselves) all require monolithic thinking and value systems—a pronounced and homogeneous management culture. Diversity is unwanted. The big machine is not only the equipment out in the operating area, but the collective psychology of those who manage its use. Change, on the other hand, tends to disturb or disrupt specific beliefs, givens, or understood values. It fragments monolithic cultures, creating diversity and allowing different opinions, methods, or alternatives to be explored.

The Lessons of Capital Investment

Whether we are describing investment in hard or soft capital, manufacturing facilities, or time-reporting systems, a few broad generalizations can be made concerning all investments. That they require fixed conditions, are expensive, and presume long, continuous payback periods is fairly obvious. That each of these factors is easily disrupted by change is equally obvious. The greater each investment, the fewer investments one can make. Each company has only so much to invest. Smaller investments allow more investments and more frequent confrontations with associated investment decisions. Larger investments mean fewer, more critical decisions. Higher technology requires higher levels of investment. Advancing technology disrupts the feasibility of any single investment once it has been made.

Investments in ideas or things create hidden impacts on our management perspectives and environments. The larger and less frequent these investments, the more singular and monolithic our culture becomes. The more we as a company have invested in the creation of the music, the instruments, and the sound stage, the more we must all sing the same song, sing it loudly, and sing it for longer periods of time. Singing, not creating music, becomes the task. Implementation skill and the willingness to comply with what has been created by others become the challenge and measure of management—how well we use the big machine.

Trading Adaptability for Efficiency

If we were just entering the business arena, in any field or capacity, the less we had invested in to-be-changed conditions, the better we would be able to cope with change. And the more uncertain we were regarding anticipated conditions, the more general our preparation would be before entering this arena. If we knew of specific risks, we could tailor and carry specific tools, but uncertainty means we're not sure what we may face.

When we invest in any one fixed idea, technique, or process in business, we should think about its transferability, its usefulness in changed conditions. In most cases this feature exacts a price. Prices of transferability (or adaptability) are commonly associated with (1) less than optimum performance in any given area, (2) a limited lifespan, (3) extra capability which may never be needed. Given the vulnerability of static capital investments in regard to change, however, most of these penalties are far less onerous than they appear.

There are other subtle and less common penalties associated with capital investments. One involves the propensity, however great, for managements to become fascinated with or intimidated by the investment itself, rather than the results the investment is supposed to bring. When a tool becomes intricate, durable, appealing in itself, we sometimes stand in awe of it, concentrating on the tool rather than the end to which it should be put. We then face the danger, in Thoreau's words, of becoming tools of our tools.

We see this in business experiences when planning teams become enamored of the plan (soft property) and neglect the use of the plan (reality), or when a management information system, task force, or project becomes some sort of a privileged corporate "pet," to be fed, guarded, and served rather than used to further business interests. The more involved any tool becomes, the more we tend to focus on it as a "noun" (something we want) rather than a "verb" (a method of getting what we want).

In other cases the mere presence of unused capacity causes us to insist on its useful employment, to make faulty business decisions in order to keep the investment running. Because of high initial cost and long, multiunit amortization requirements, the need to feed the machine, to make continued use of it, becomes a powerful driving force. Changes that make use of the machine questionable are often overlooked in our haste to keep it "on line," "at peak capacity," or "contributing." When a business investment *drives* the business (rather than *serving* it), it ceases to become an asset. Regardless of what the financial statements say, the investment becomes a management liability.

The Unstoppable DC-3

The airplane that pioneered commercially viable passenger service in the 1930s was the DC-3, created by the Douglas Airplane Company (later MacDonell-Douglas). Today, after over 50 years of aviation innovation and revolutionary technical advances in aircraft performance, there are still over 1000 DC-3s in commercial operation—this despite the fact that, compared with modern equipment, the DC-3 is a slow, noisy, uncomfortable aircraft. How can this be?

The DC-3 simply allows businesses to enter the air-carrying field with minimum investment and to operate with minimum *investment-driven constraints*. An overhauled, certified DC-3 suitable for cargo or passenger services costs around $125,000, as compared with several million dollars for comparable new equipment. Marginal routes and small loads are profitable, and more important, the machine doesn't demand that the owner's business keep it flying constantly in order to amortize the cost. It can sit on runways for hours, even days. It can access small fields, it can make low-margin cargo profitable, and it can *wait*. This explains why it is a well-regarded favorite of small entrepreneurial operators. It assists their operations rather than determining what the operations will be and how they will be performed. It is one airplane that doesn't drive the company but serves it.

Since an appropriate business response to change is to become lean in investment and agile in pursuit of opportunity, we can use counterparts to the DC-3 in many other industries. If the concepts of freedom from tools and agility in the face of change needed a mascot or a symbol, we could do no better than to choose this machine. And if the world needed a symbol of the opposite, of massive, recalcitrant, complex, fixed, dependent, and business-driving investment, we could do no better than to choose a modern nuclear power plant under construction—any one of them. Now there's an industry that could use a counterpart to the DC-3!

Living with Less

Given the penalties of massive capital investment, how should we operate under changed conditions? First of all, we will probably see less investment per idea, less capital devoted to any single endeavor. More and more companies will be mitigating risk by spreading their capacity among several efforts, the so-called portfolio effect. Those enterprises or pursuits chosen for investment will be required to become productive quickly, avoiding the cost and risk of obsolescence associated with long "construction" periods. Limited, phased commitments will be made as managements edge into pursuits step by step, rather than taking the giant, irrevocable leaps seen in the past.

Technological commitments, except in specialized areas, will be limited and short-term. No one today wants to sign a 20-year computer lease. Premiums will be placed on adaptable technology, items that can defy or delay the impacts of change as much as possible (see Chapter 3). Management apparatus (reporting systems, organizations, procedures, etc.) will be simple and goal-oriented rather than complex, rote, and prescriptive. To the extent possible, management apparatus will be independent of conditions which may change, such as specific personnel, using location, or application.

Because fixed assets are vulnerable ones, we will see more partial or temporary commitments for tools and people (leases, rentals, temporary work forces, consultants, etc.) and more investment in changeable assets—assets that can be easily liquefied. Chief among these are cash and people. The shift from investment in apparatus to investment in people will become more pronounced, because people are much more flexible, adaptive, and change-sensitive than are hard or soft properties.

When the upsetting impact of change is fully considered, we may reverse our classic view of capital investment from a focus on the benefits it brings to a cognizance of the liabilities it embodies. It may be that, all factors considered, less *is* more.

Developing Contrasts

Sometimes the best way to detect change is to see contrasts between the old and the new, the past and the present, or what tendencies or features seem to be developing as businesses move through time. As we explore this and the remaining business responses to change, then, it will prove useful to isolate certain contrasting elements that serve to point out emerging differences in our workplaces and among our managements. We shall do this by listing a particular set of contrasting elements, not because they alone demonstrate the effects of change, but only to illustrate, for some aspects of business, the deepening gaps between what sufficed in times of fixity and what is needed to accommodate times of change. This first set consists of contrasts between the presumptions needed to invest large sums in capital and the reality created by change.

Investment Presumptions	*Reality of Change*
Stable resources	Fluctuating price and availability
Dependable markets	Markets in transition
Bigger is better	Less is more
Batch production	Custom productions
Increased efficiency	Need for adaptability
Firm commitments	Tentative, partial commitments
Stationary technology	Technology in flux
Lengthy payback periods	Fleeting exploitation opportunity

The Prices and Risks of Capital Shedding

The notion that less extensive capital investment may be a better way to cope with a changing world is not without its prices and risks. As with each of the management trends we shall examine in this volume, this one can be carried to extremes, misinterpreted, or misapplied. Even when used judiciously and appropriately, certain inherent risks are involved and must be addressed.

No one should shed capitalization to the extent that viable, profitable enterprises are constantly undercapitalized or underequipped simply because, as a concept, capitalization is viewed as evil. We need to fully support those efforts that are contributing to our companies for as long as they contribute. We should, however, be a bit more careful and deliberate in how we support each and how retractable such commitments can be. In other words, we should invest piecemeal where we can, for short horizon periods, and only insofar as payback can be foreseen. We should feed our ideas a month or a quarter at a time, and avoid buying 5 years' supply of food. Even the healthiest of ideas may die before the food is exhausted.

A bias against extensive capital investment carries with it the risk that any one enterprise will not be fully exploited, fully optimized. This is a true penalty, one that cannot be denied. It must be said, however, that marginal gains not made by further exploitation of any one opportunity can be offset by major gains in other areas—areas made available by the excess investment not used in the first area. Put in other terms, most companies would rather have three opportunities exploited at 75 percent than one exploited at 99 percent.

Less capitalization or more prudent, selective investment relies upon more and more planning, study, and analysis. A lot more looking is needed before one takes a leap. Infatuation with planning as an end and not a tool is possible unless steps are taken to prevent it. All planning, studies, and the like should proceed in incremental fashion, step by step, as increased feasibility potential dictates. We should invest in plans piecemeal, just as we should invest in opportunities. The attraction of planning (rather than simply taking the plunge into reality) is that plans can be revoked, are relatively inexpensive, and do not tie up company resources. Plunging ahead with unmerited capital investments is just the opposite.

Reluctant investment in view of change means fewer and fewer megaprojects—fewer giant power plants, space missions, massive social programs, long-term research efforts. To be sure, these will still be undertaken, but not nearly as frequently or with such initial carte blanche freedom as in the past, in times when the debilitating effects of change were not as well recognized. The problem with megaprojects is that they are so vulnerable to changed conditions, require so much investment, and take so long to return results that they are unable to withstand the tests of their own time frames. Tomorrow's projects will be smaller, shorter, less capital-intensive, and more promising of quick paybacks. Megaprojects require stable conditions, sustained dedication of resources, and goals or intentions of a higher order than dictated by economics. In the future these will include only wars or their moral equivalents.

With shorter and shorter projects, more frequent evaluation and justification of feasibility, and less patient payback expectations, managements of tomorrow's efforts will have little time for the luxury of fixed conditions. Those wishing to settle back, find a home, or relax in the comforting niche of a long-term effort will have to look far and wide to find a spot. Managers in changing times must get comfortable with the notion of change, not with unchanged conditions.

If larger, more irrevocable capital investments mean fewer and more centralized ones, then the converse should be true. This means that less investment per idea or opportunity should lead to more frequent, more decentralized decision making on the part of company managements. In addition, we will have to consider goals and products at the end of the process more frequently than is done at present. Rather than remain infatuated with the development and use of properties, our managers must more frequently lift their heads from the machinery and consider why it exists, or whether it should exist at all.

A final caution regarding this trend is needed. Some managements may take the reluctance to invest to an extreme, shying away from or actually fearing commitment even when it is merited. Simply because we must be more prudent with limited investments and pursue carefully selected opportunities is not a reason to avoid the many opportunities that surely exist. Carried to an extreme, prudent commitment can be interpreted as no commitment, a failure to commit at all in view of the potential of change-derived failure.

No capitalization means no business. The message here is not that capitalization is a mistake, but that, considering the impact of change and the conditions favoring capitalization, it makes no sense to bear the *burden of capitalization* any more than absolutely necessary.

3

Choosing Shields
Over Targets

Designing for change immunity

*With a simple framework we can begin to
make sense of the world. And we can change
that framework as the world changes.*
JOHN NAISBITT

The phenomenon of businesschange is causing us to rethink the way we plan and select our products and services. *Designing for change* will soon rank next to designing for function, for form, or for customer acceptance. As with the analyses made here, it is easier to detect this business response to change when applied to products rather than services or other "soft properties" such as procedures, policy, organizations, or plans. So too is it easier to detect physical signposts of change-driven design, no matter what form it takes, as the key to the future. Here are some of those signposts which are now appearing, or about to appear, on the business horizon.

Signposts of Change

- *A proliferation of disposable products.* We've seen disposable watches, lighters, razors, flashlights, and the like. Look for disposable eyeglasses, neckties, vacuum cleaners, luggage, and electronics. The old notions of "cheap" and "waste" are taking on a new meaning.

- **More modular components and plug-in repairs.**   Major appliances will offer do-it-yourself repair kits and tollfree advice. Shoes are coming with extra soles attached by velcro strips. The repair shop of the future will be the home.

- **Basic products offering multiple upgrade options.**   Computer boards, hard disks, and modems all help upgrade and enhance a fairly basic product. Automobile "options" have always been "upgrade kits." Aftermarket sales are big and getting bigger, for a multitude of products.

- **Marketing emphasis on multiple product uses.**   Arm and Hammer baking soda pioneered the way. Other companies are following suit.

- **The stressing of timelessness and endurance for prestige items.**   Consider Mont Blanc pens and Dupont lighters. And Mercedes-Benz now offers a 4-year warranty, while Jaguars are warranted for 3 years.

- **Rapid dissemination of fashion through the middle class.**   Off-price stores, discount houses, and mass label consciousness are shortening the time and dollar spans between fashion leaders and fashion laggards. And of course, television is the great leveler of fashion awareness. In a world of multiple choices, the assurance of a brand name is often critical.

- **Management emphasis on basics rather than business fads.**   Note the recent abandonment of high-flying buzzwords ("strategic plans," "integration of information," "matrix meshing," and "closed-loop process methodology") and the reappearance of simple, yet powerful terminology in today's management vocabulary: "leading," "listening," "showing," "rewarding," "control," "ability").

- **The disappearance of "new" and "improved" from the advertising lexicon.**   Look for more specific accolades, particularly those denoting opposite poles—endurance and frivolity, seriousness and spontaneity—and the notions of "classic," "dependable," "reliable," "quality," and "complete."

The Beauty of Change Immunity

One of the highest compliments we can give a person, a company, or a product is to say that it is "timeless," that it endures, persists unmodified through vastly differing conditions—that it is *immune to change.* We value the ability of anything to thrive in change, to remain unruffled and undamaged even when it must exist in a windstorm of change.

As the forces and avenues of change multiply and increase in importance, the value of those features, attitudes, and approaches that thrive in change increases. A major challenge of any management effort, therefore, is to design our products, companies, and approaches so that they are as timeless, or immune to change, as possible. In this chapter we explore the notion of change immunity as it pertains to business activity and results; ways to enhance change immunity in everything we do; and, just as important, ways to spot *change targets*—those elements of our makeup or activity that make us susceptible to the ravages of change. Our goal in a changing world is to create change shields and remove needless change targets.

The Concept of Change Design

When we address ways to design for change immunity, our focus will be very broad, covering any element of design and any object thereof. We shall consider not only classic product design, engineering design, architecture, fashion, or utility as it applies to produced objects but also the role of design as it pertains to management activity and tools. We do in fact design such things as reporting systems; organizational arrangements; job functions; long- and short-range plans; management information systems; and a whole range of management approaches, techniques, and control scaffolding. Although the object of change design may vary, the concept remains valid. We should let nothing we do escape the scrutiny of a change-conscious consideration, and let no candidates for change immunity go unnoticed.

Several qualities can be described as closely related to or synonomous with change immunity. Among these is "durability," or resistance to failure, degradation, or loss of utility. The more durable a product or concept, the more change-immune it becomes. Consequently, something that can be easily repaired, strengthened, or restored is more apt to be called "timeless" or "immune to change," particularly if it is immune to the degradation brought about through use or time itself. Whenever maintenance is simple and inexpensive, replacement elements are widely available and uniform, and accessories can be added to expand the utility of an item, the item becomes more immune to change, more timeless. Any item with multiple uses has a built-in portfolio quality, so to speak, which gives it more and more chances to remain valid and useful (time-

less) despite changes which may render certain capabilities or uses in-
valid.

Durability, repairability, and multiplicity of use, then, are features
making physical products less susceptible to the ravages of time, wear,
and changing needs. These are fairly easy to visualize when we think of
hard objects—things we can see, touch, and "fix." It takes more abstract
visualization, though, to apply these to *soft properties*—intangibles, or
things that cannot easily be seen and touched. These include plans,
approaches, techniques, and processes—the bag of tricks used by most
business managers in their daily work.

The Ravages of Change: Two Responses

There are a number of other ways we can protect something from the
degradation or obsolescence that changes surely bring. Here we will
examine two major approaches taken by many businesses. These involve
the features called "disposability" and, in the other extreme, "endurance." While physical objects will be used to illustrate each approach,
keep in mind that they both are constantly applied, consciously or not,
to more abstract, soft properties.

We can withstand the effects of change or persist despite its activity
if our products endure, if their design and construction embody strength,
quality, simplicity, and immunity to the whims of fashion, among other
attributes. To attain endurance we must invest heavily in the product,
making it of strong material, using dependable components and reliable
construction or fabrication methods, and maintaining the requisite train
of spare parts, maintenance, and service capabilities. Enduring products
lean into the wind of change, welcoming the challenge, confident they
will persist with little damage. Products designed to endure take themselves very seriously.

Just the opposite approach is taken with disposable products. They
require minimum investment, for both the producer and the consumer,
and frequently make use of temporary, cheap, and fragile components
and unskilled or automated labor. These products readily admit their
weakness, their lack of endurance; but by their very nature, they suggest
that it doesn't matter if they are struck down by time or change, they
can be discarded with little loss. They can then be repurchased, or re-
created in a different mold, one more applicable to current conditions.
Disposable products shed the burden of capitalization; they are cheap
and temporary, and they laugh at themselves. Were we to expect anything more, we could be missing the point of disposability. Disposability

is a valuable concept that is employed quite well for a number of products we use every day. And these products bring profit to people who understand the concept of disposability.

Watches and Razors

Take the common wristwatch as a case in point. Although fashions and the technology of time regulation have changed and will continue to do so, we can point to specific wristwatch designs as good examples of how different approaches to the question of change immunity translate to items with which we are familiar.

Consider the famous Rolex Oyster Perpetual watches sold throughout the world. Compare them with the ubiquitous inexpensive, plastic, battery-driven "computer chip" watches on the other end of the price spectrum, such as the Swatch brand. These products take vastly different tacks toward the phenomenon of change. The Rolex is expensive, well made, precise, accurate, strong, and *enduring*. It endures for two reasons: (1) each watch is so well designed and crafted that its physical makeup lasts for decades (it seldom wears out or breaks), and (2) its design and appearance transcend momentary fluctuations of wristwatch fashion. The basic look of such a watch has been virtually unaltered for generations, yet it is still regarded as attractive, smart, and fashionable throughout the world.

Way down at the other end of the wristwatch scale, we find the "plastic chips." All are inexpensive, nondurable, and disposable. Rather than endure the ravages of time, or transcend them as does the Rolex, these products can be easily "sacrificed" to the god of change, to the force of time. They can be tossed away without many tears whenever they (1) break or (2) become unfashionable. Since their initial cost (investment) is so minor, an average consumer can afford to buy a new one as frequently as he or she wishes. Then too, a very inexpensive item need not be backed up by an expensive pipeline of replacement parts, detailed upgrading components, or comprehensive service and warranty provisions. If it breaks we simply toss it away. Why spend $100 in time and expense trying to fix a $10 item?

Disposable watches can afford to follow the whims and fancies of fashion to the extreme. They can set the fashion trends, be as bold and "fashionable" as they like, for they seldom endure beyond the next fashion turn anyway. Again, a newer, more currently fashionable model is easy to obtain once the outmoded version is disposed of.

The Resistance of Symbols

Once something becomes a symbol of a higher, less changeable quality or feature, it gains in change immunity. This is because although the object itself may appear outmoded, the symbol it represents is not. Take *success*, for example. The trappings of success vary from one period to the next (what symbolizes success; what a successful person owns, does, believes, etc.), but the concept of success and the desire to attain it remain fairly constant.

If a Rolex watch becomes a symbol of success, therefore, the symbol retains value and currency even though the physical object which projects it becomes dated. After all, there are just as accurate (or more so), equally attractive, and much less expensive wristwatches on the market; but there are few which project or symbolize so many desirable qualities, such as achievement, discretionary income, consciousness of quality, strength, dependability, and timelessness.

This is why many physical symbols of success are considered timeless or "classic" even though their utilitarian value is limited or reduced by change. Countless examples exist, including automobiles, antique furniture, artwork, literature, and jewelry. Most people can readily appreciate the value of a beautifully preserved Louis XIV chair, yet how many of us would be willing to use it to seat Uncle Tiny for an all-night poker game? Better to offer him an orange crate, and quickly dispose of it once the game is over.

Disposable products are not without symbolism of their own. Because they can readily adapt (or be replaced by those which adapt) to twists and turns in the world of fashion, they symbolize or declare to the world that their wearers are fashionable, that they are conscious of and participants in the fashion of the day. These products also symbolize adaptability, egalitarianism, or (in their less than fashionable designs) functional utilitarianism.

Status Symbols in the Closet

There are other examples of disposability besides watches. If we consider safety razors, we will uncover similar reactions to the design of change immunity. The difference between watches and razors is the power and value of a visible symbol as compared with an object that few other people see. Few of us carry our safety razors around for all to see, there to represent us or indicate our position, taste, or wealth. Safety razors generally stay hidden in the privacy of our bathrooms. Thus, the element of symbolism, particularly regarding the status of the owner, is weak and of little value.

A well-made and enduring razor does reconfirm a person's personal taste, values, or whatever, but usually only in private—not to others. If we wish to emphasize the razor as a status symbol, then, we must focus primarily on those times when it is viewed by others: when it is purchased and (if a gift) when it is given. It is interesting to see how this distinction makes its way into advertising.

How Cheap is "Cheap"?

If there is one lesson the Japanese and other foreign competitors have taught American business leaders, it is to reevaluate our old notions of "cheap" and "waste" when applied to certain product designs. The Bic pen, the disposable razor, the plastic cigarette lighter, and the inflatable spare tire are items that, while each appears less enduring than its durable counterpart, make elegant sense. After consumers got over their initial image of "cheapness," they became accustomed to the utilitarian logic behind their development. How did the resulting wholehearted acceptance of disposability happen?

The answer lies in the *purpose* of these items as opposed to any inherent value they may project by virtue of their design and construction. A lighter's purpose is to light, a razor's to shave, a pen's to write, and a spare tire's to provide emergency service. Other features not critical to these purposes have been wisely deemed secondary or even nonessential. What most American manufacturers failed to realize, as they continued to market enduring products, often selling at 10 times the price, was that function, not feature, is central to the purchasing decision. If a plastic lighter will provide light after light without a cumbersome maintenance chain of spare flints, refill liquid, and periodic case repair, isn't it a good alternative to the traditional hard, heavy, large, and more enduring Zippo? People who claim that the periodic disposal of otherwise working parts when the Bic runs out of fluid represents waste should consider the waste of millions of fluid cans and flint dispensers, and thousands of hours of hinge repair labor. It's also fair to speculate that, considering the unused metal of older twin-edged safety blades and the necessary metal containers in which they are packaged, the disposable razor actually represents a net savings in material and manufacturing energy. Here lies a major principle of change-resistant design: disposability as a design concept often *reduces* net waste.

The inflatable spare tire provides another example. Think of the waste involved in millions of automobiles hauling around millions of never-to-be-used full-size spare tires and wheels! We don't carry spare batteries, spare fuel pumps, or spare oil filters—why tires? Full-size tires in trunks simply give the assurance of "endurance" and protection to those who somehow need it. Considering the extra material and fuel wasted, not to mention larger automobiles or smaller trunks, this false assurance is perhaps the biggest "waste" of all.

Each of these products has changed because its designers took a hard look at what was contributing and what wasn't, and at how each factor was affected by change. They improved parts subject to wear or made them disposable, and they purposely "designed out" those elements that, although giving the appearance of endurance and value, actually detracted from change immunity in the finished item. It's fair to say there are a great number of other products we now take for granted in their size, shape, and composition that could benefit from this pragmatic, change-conscious design. Your products may be among them.

Do-It-Yourself Resoles

A manufacturer of running shoes, Turntec, has recently carried the concept of change-immune design a step further (pardon the pun). Noting that the outsole (the part hitting the pavement) of most running shoes wears out long before the rest, Turntec has come out with a novel alternative. A new model has interchangeable soles that can be fastened and unfastened with a special, tough, Velcro-type mechanism. When the first outsole wears out, the owner simply rips it off and replaces it with a new one—at home, with no special tools or adhesives.

The design actually goes farther. In addition to prolonging shoe life (*repairability*) it allows different soles to be used, at will, for different athletic purposes (*multiplicity of purposes*). A runner who also bicycles, for example, can slap on a special, stiff, cleated biking sole and avoid the cost of a separate pair of shoes made especially for that purpose. The replaceable sole handles change in two distinct ways: (1) it sacrifices a disposable sole to wear-induced change, and (2) it adapts to changes in the wearer's sport.

Sacrifice and Protection

The concept of disposability also applies to objects or soft properties in which symbolism, fashion, and images have absolutely no place, in which sensibility and utility reign supreme. Take the problem of decomposition of buried metal tanks, for example. In the past, these were subject to extreme corrosion, rusting away because of water and chemicals acting upon them underground (caused by the physical ravages of time and change). Insightful designers determined that "sacrificial elements" could be attached to these tanks to circumvent the corrosion by attracting it, so to speak, to themselves and deflecting the effects from the tank. Using the practice called "cathodic protection" in this way, sacrificial cathodes and anodes are placed alongside buried tanks to bear the brunt of the corrosion. This is a no-nonsense example of disposable design.

We see other examples of the concepts of sacrificial parts or endurance all around us. Tools which have replaceable cutting edges or wearing surfaces utilize the idea of disposability. Those with tempered or hardened wearing surfaces take the opposite approach, putting endurance at the points that are most subjected to the ravages of change.

Designing for endurance means: (1) large initial investments; (2) little need for repair or maintenance and ease of both when required; (3) the ability to dictate, evade, or somehow transcend fashion; and (4) the use of special symbolism to deflect the impacts of change from the projecting object. Designing for disposability means: (1) little initial investment; (2) disposal and replacement rather than repair or maintenance; (3) the freedom to follow or to set fashion; and (4) use of special symbolism, in certain cases, to emphasize the attributes of disposability (adaptability, fashion consciousness, capriciousness, independence from convention, etc.).

The Sharp Edge of Fashion

By and large, those products that require substantial investment and are high-fashion, for example, don't fare too well. Except for the exceedingly rich, the ability to follow fashion closely is tied to the ability to turn over our personal inventory of fashionable products once they have fallen out of favor and replace them with newer, currently fashionable counterparts. We simply can't buy a new mink coat every season.

Herein lies the very meaning of the term "fashionable." It describes people who are able to follow fashion (hence "fashion-able") and is useful to them because it *distinguishes* them from the rest, from those not able (because of taste, income, or other constraints) to keep up with the latest. This is why even the most fashionable item falls out of favor with people on the leading edge of fashion as soon as it is adopted by the masses. Any item loses value for the fashionable whenever it fails to distinguish them and, instead, makes them more like the rest of society. This is the point in time when whatever was "in" quickly becomes "out."

Alligators as Change Targets

A classic example of change targets in the fashion world involves the Izod line of clothing, noted for its conspicuous alligator emblem. A fairly little known product for decades, the knit tennis shirt sporting the alligator was favored by a small but affluent set of buyers. During the early 1980s the alligator burst into popularity, and Izod sales shot up dramatically. An alligator on one's shirt became the statement of fashionable sportswear, and retailers had trouble keeping up with the demand.

Izod leveraged the drawing power of the alligator by sewing it onto associated products, and the reptile's eyes soon peered out from socks, belts, trousers, ties, and jackets. The alligator was on a big roll, and dozens of other companies followed its lead, resulting in an entire menagerie of creatures (bears, penguins, tigers, horses, hogs, and every other animal imaginable) adorning competitive products. And suddently, just after this fashion trend had peaked, it took a plummet.

The Izod nosedive could have been predicted by anyone familiar with the notion of change targets, particularly as they relate to fashion. If we wanted to select a single product as a symbol of a change target, the once-proud alligator would be a fine choice. Once it mutated from a special symbol for a privileged few to a ubiquitous presence among the middle and lower classes, its days were numbered. The feature that initially made it so popular, so *today*, was the same one that made it so tired, so *yesterday*, once it stopped distinguishing the fashion leaders from the fashion laggards. It then mutated from a change champion to a change target, from an asset to a liability. It was even common for people to slice the alligators off their shirts in order to avoid the appearance of being 2 years behind the leading edge of fashion. A company's ride atop a wave of change can be thrilling and profitable, but it is perilous as well. Just ask any alligator.

What Else Works?

Besides disposability and endurance, other design features shore up a product, or a soft property, against the effects of potential change. Interchangeability is one such feature. If an object has many uses, or is a good substitute for a number of other products, it may remain valid as long as any one of these uses is required. Baking soda is an example.

Originally used only in baking or as a substitute for tooth powder, it has now found utility as a freshener of refrigerators, carpets, and pet bedding. We can even use it for medicinal purposes. Since home baking is declining today and consumers are attracted to specific, multifeatured toothpastes, sales of baking soda might be expected to decline. However, its rediscovered medicinal value and freshening capabilities (its multiple uses) keep it a very active, change-immune item. Multiple uses not only enhance sales but also prolong them over changing times. Like a chameleon, a product with multiple uses simply transforms its utility as changing values and circumstances dictate.

An item's capability for being upgraded or modified also prevents it from becoming timeworn, obsolete, or outgrown. Computer manufacturers know this well, as do those who sell audio and video equipment. An often-forgotten version of product upgrade concerns product trade-in, most commonly seen with automobiles.

Closely associated with the notion of multiple uses is product (or concept) versatility, the capability of an object for use for its intended purpose but under different circumstances. Power tools which operate on direct current or with battery packs are therefore more versatile than those which operate in only one way.

As for fashion immunity, those items which do not either track along— or worse, exaggerate—the peaks and valleys of fashion's course seem to fare better over the long run than those that ride the fashion roller coaster. Understatement endures the vicissitudes of fashion better than overstatement does.

Timeless Books and Movies

We can even extend the concept of timelessness into the businesses of storytelling, book writing, and moviemaking. In these areas, to create a product that can be enjoyed for years to come, one must carefully avoid change targets as well; references which needlessly date the material and tie it to a specific time frame. Timeless fiction, for example, withstands changes among its readers because it focuses on unchanging values, struggles, and emotions, not on current or contemporary fashion, fad, or popular whim. And here again, the features and characteristics which make a work so topical, so compelling, so important *today* are often the same ones which make the same work so dated, so tired, and so inappropriate *tomorrow*.

Designing Management Apparatus

The impact of changing fashion in areas other than clothing, literature, and entertainment may not be immediately apparent, but it is nevertheless felt. We suffer under its whims and capriciousness in the world of business as well, for management approaches, objectives, techniques, and tools can also be either enduring or disposable (or those failed gradations in between), and can be interchangeable, versatile, modular, or not. When we try to relate the concept of design for change immunity to these areas, we can use what applies to physical objects just as well. What works (or fails) for wristwatches and razors also works (or fails) for strategic plans, project organizations, and management information systems.

What this all means to people who create management tools and enunciate management ideals is that, by spending a little more time and effort on the front end of their creation, and by considering change as a major design challenge, they can save countless dollars, days, and headaches in the future.

Developing Contrasts

One way to summarize a growing understanding of the ways we can avoid change damage by designing around it is to contrast *change targets* with *change shields*.

Change Targets	Change Shields
Reliance on fads	Projection of lasting symbols
Personality dependence	Functional dependence
Single use	Multiple uses
Technology dependence	Technology transcendence
Degrading elements	Sacrificial or hardened elements
Fashion's leading edge	Fashion's center, or above fashion
One condition, one capability	Upgrading to many capabilities

The Prices and Risks of Change Immunity

The practice of designing for change immunity—like shedding the burden of capitalization and many of the other responses to the phenomenon of change addressed in this book—carries special risks and prices. These vary depending upon the nature of each business, its management objectives, and the specific design approaches taken.

Companies that take the endurance route, that stress quality and timelessness through higher capital investment in the product and associated features, may thereby miss an opportunity to exploit short-term fads and fashions. This sort of opportunity is actually minor, however; and although each such opportunity may make someone an instant millionaire, these opportunities come about infrequently, are highly dependent on timing, and are totally unpredictable.

Endurance and its attendant diminishing of "newness," fashion, or fad cannot rely upon the alluring features most products seem to treasure. These deal with the traditional selling power of a product that is viewed as new, improved, or technologically advanced. On second thought, however, the value of "new" as a descriptive term may itself be changing. In the past, the term conveyed improvement, advancement, modernity. Whatever was new was automatically more valuable than whatever it made "old," even its own previous version. But sometimes, especially today, the connotation of "newness" is not always positive. If something is called "new" today, this might imply it is untested, questionable, experimental, artificial, too complex, full of unknown side effects, and the like. "New" need not equate to "good." It can mean "bad."

Companies not vertically integrated or not associated with aftermarket products may also be reluctant to design change immunity through replaceable parts, components, or modules. They may be more interested, or only interested, in selling the entire product. Those making several closely related products may not follow the principle of planning for versatility, which might mean that purchase of one of their products would eliminate the need for many others. Such companies may choose instead to highlight specific products for specific needs, the distinctions among each being highly featured. Similarly, companies which rely upon service, such as repair work, for a major portion of their income are generally not inclined to sponsor production of disposable units which make repair a moot issue.

Certain observations in this chapter also apply well to managerial products or services. Newly appointed executives have a fondness for change, for making their mark on the effort, for bringing in "newness." They are often reluctant to emphasize the enduring qualities of whatever it is they wish to replace. Those wishing to promote capital ventures (new products) often discredit or reduce the value of upgrading existing operations or finding other uses for existing capabilities (versatility). Many other similar analogies can be made. As our discussion of typical reactions to change continues, we will uncover several.

4

Letting Results Drive for a Change

Placing purpose before process

To observe processes and to construct means is science; to criticize and coordinate ends is philosophy. . . . For a fact is nothing except in relation to desire; it is not complete except in relation to a purpose and a whole.

WILL DURANT

An action or a pursuit is termed "teleological" if it pertains to a purpose or a goal. The response to businesschange discussed in this chapter fits that term, for an unmistakable trait of change consciousness is the habit of looking at results before means, at destinations before routes, and at purposes before processes aimed at achieving them. A purpose-driven company first chooses where it wants to be, and only then creates the mechanism and the path for getting there.

A management shift from process to purpose orientations is often a significant, even revolutionary, change, but it typically has subtle, suggestive indications. For this reason, the signposts of such a shift are usually not as dramatic as the shift itself. Here are some indicators we now see.

Signposts of Change

- *A larger number of redundant manufacturing or production systems.* Make it inside or buy it outside. Switch lines, switch batches, make it remotely and assemble it here, make it here and assemble it remotely. More alternatives give us more protection from change in any one system.

- *Fewer avoidable process or resource dependencies.* Energy has been the key variable here. Alternative power sources and alternative material requirements yield production and service flexibility.

- *More frequent outsourcing alternatives for components.* More subassembly identification, more subcontractor choices, and less reluctance to look outside for capacity.

- *More flexible production lines with more soft links.* Computer-aided design and computer-assisted manufacturing (CAD and CAM) hold out tremendous promise.

- *Emergence of "process experts."* The discipline of process design and control will expand to virtually every field of business.

- *Less emphasis on basic research.* This is unfortunate, but predictable. When opportunity is fleeting, companies want results quicker. Applied research is seen as more responsive. Green and Berry explain the difference: "Devoted exclusively to creating new knowledge, basic research generally is long term in scope and yields uncertain payoff. Applied research, by contrast, pursues specific, practical and commercial aims. It is less chancy than basic research, although the payoff may not be as big" (1985, p. 128).

- *Less patience with lengthy development efforts.* If an item takes too long to conceive, analyze, study, design, prototype, test, and produce, it won't be approved. The bottom line still exists; it is simply moving up the page.

- *More incomplete, unfinished, untested concepts reaching markets too soon.* The urgency of timing will result in premature deliveries. Smart buyers will avoid the first model series. Whatever we buy that is new will simply have more bugs in it. The consumer is becoming the producer's quality control department.

- *Emphasis on management by objectives, not by activity.* Executives will push for results of work rather than level of effort. Working long and hard won't count; working smart and producing results, regardless of the means, will count.

- *More frequent measurement of accomplishment (feedback).* The pressures of time and change make us crave information about intermediate progress. We won't be able to wait until we finish to see how well we did. We will create milestones and projections all along the way.

Process: The Means of Inducing Change

Everyone involved in business, in no matter what industry or position, is a participant to one degree or another in some sort of process. Indeed, a business is nothing more than a series or collection of processes aimed at changing what is not initially useful, in some context, to what is useful. Virtually every management effort, technique, or system is ultimately process-oriented—existing to further some desired process or group of processes.

A process is no more than that which converts what we have to what we want (or what someone else wants). This conversion, the essence of all business enterprises, produces the *value added* as a result of our work. We begin our effort with an initial set of expectations (what we want to achieve), perform a process (what we "do"), and end with some sort of desired results. The active agent we employ as part of any process is *change*, converting expectations to results. This relationship can be expressed thusly:

$$\text{Expectations + resources} \xrightarrow{\textit{induced change}} \text{results}$$

This broad definition of a process is easy to apply to almost everything done in business, at all levels and in all areas. A shipping clerk who sees to it that boxes of goods located in a warehouse are transferred, in proper quantity and type, to waiting vehicles is managing a process. In this case, the process is one of changing stored material to material ready to be transferred from storage. In a small but essential way, the clerk adds value to the stored material by placing it on transport vehicles. The resources are changed from the stored to the shippable condition, adding benefit as a result of this simple process.

The driver who conveys the material from the warehouse to the retail store adds value in turn by converting goods in a wholesale condition to goods available for retail sale, again using change (in a spatial sense associated with distribution) to perform a process. The shipping clerk and the driver each perform small processes (subprocesses) which, when linked together, complete an overall business process.

In another example of a necessary process employing change (here in both condition and location) to add value, a farmer uses various tools and knowledge to convert growing wheat plants in a field to stored grain in an elevator. An advertising agency that increases consumer demand for or knowledge of a finished product (say bread) uses various processes to change an unknown product to one that is known and in demand. A carpentry crew that changes a truckload of lumber into a precisely crafted formwork for use in concrete construction also uses a process to convert resources to expectations. A print shop changes a promoter's idea into usable handbills fit for distribution, making use of many processes to convert what exists (ideas, expectations, paper, ink) into what is desired (finished handbills).

Squirrels in Cages

We must be careful to discern the difference between raw, simple activity and the activity essential to the conversion processes we depend upon. Activity is not productive unless it is a necessary element of one or more processes.

To use an analogy, we can think of raw activity as the motion of a squirrel in a cage. As the animal runs and runs within a spinning exercise wheel, it performs a good deal of activity, but it gets nowhere. Were we to hook the wheel to an electrical generation device, however, the squirrel and its activity would become a linked element of a productive process. As we look at the different activities in our business environments, we may be somewhat surprised to see how many of them are non-process-oriented, like the activity of the squirrel on the wheel—how many of them are simply motions with no process justification.

Harnessing Change

No business could exist without change, for it is through change that resources are converted to results. Earlier it was stated that change is nonexistent without effects; the same can be said of processes. Processes without effects are not processes at all, but empty activity. And because any change can have many effects, some predicted and some not, the same is true of any process.

We often view a process with the same misconceptions as those with which we sometimes view change—that is, we expect the process to be linear, direct, and repeatable. Except in the most basic and rare cases, this is not true. Like change, processes have many effects, some anticipated and some not. Even those anticipated often count for more than that which we value or want to encourage—the affective essence of each process. Many side effects, spinoffs, and nonvalued results accompany the results we profit from. These undesirables are the inconsequential *noise* and the consequential *penalties* resulting from our conversion processes—from our work.

Harnessing change to further a process is much like harnessing stored energy; it brings negative as well as positive results. When we burn fuel oil to heat our houses, we also disrupt the atmosphere (pollution), deplete our household budgets (price of oil), wear out our oil-burning apparatus, produce excess local heat not needed, raise our risk of fire, increase our dependency on fuel oil deliveries, increase the incidence of spills and cleanup problems, and produce many other detrimental effects that are part and parcel of the processes needed to gain one sought-after effect: warmth in our homes. No change happens in a vacuum. Each has wanted and unwanted results: value and price. Sometimes the prices of our business processes are direct and noticeable, and often the noise and penalties associated with them are unknown, secondary, and detrimental.

Any manager who looks simply at the selected effects of change, at the process contribution and not at the noise and penalties of that process, is missing the character of change. Such a manager is guilty of focusing only on the *managed variable*, the harnessed effects of change, and of not being totally aware of the holistic nature of the phenomenon. Change works for us and against us, and most often does both at the same time.

Process Vulnerabilities

Business managers becoming more and more aware of the nature and function of change, then, must confront each process under their purview and examine the role of change therein. When we do this we typically find that change is both friend and foe and that the unwanted effects of change can be eliminated or mitigated by reconfiguring and redirecting the process itself. That is, we need to evaluate each process to determine how susceptible it may be to the noise and penalties of change, how vulnerable it is. Process improvements, therefore, involve not only optimization (better use of change as a controlled phenomenon), but shielding of the process from noise and penalties spun off from the beneficial change agent, and from the unplanned action of unharnessed change. An ideal process not only works well but works consistently, continuously, and dependably—protected, as it were, from the vagaries of unwanted change and unplanned change effects.

If we think of each element of a process as a potential vulnerability, nonessential elements (unproductive activity) become change targets in the process. They enlarge our profile, giving change more opportunity to interfere without adding value. Change targets abound in virtually every process, just as they do in many product designs (see Chapter 3).

The king of process vulnerability has to be inflexibility. Any time a process includes "only one way" of doing something, only one method of conversion, we have restricted our ability to circumvent change. If our process has several parallel paths, allowing us to convert needs to results in many different ways, depending on not only what's optimum but what's available under the circumstances, we have a process shielded from change.

Shifting Our Eyes from the Route to the Destination

The key feature of a change-resistant process is its constant emphasis on *destination* over particular *route*, on what we want achieved (result) over how we go about achieving it (process). Were it not for change, this would be unnecessary. We could fix every variable needing fixity, manipulate the active ones, and perform consistent and ever more efficient conversion. Change keeps us from doing this; we must constantly reexamine the effectiveness of each process as it is affected by changing conditions, relationships, and objectives. The more flexible and results-oriented a process becomes, the more viable it is in a changing world. The same is true of business managers.

It's easy to see a failed or imperfect process: (1) It has a preponderance of nonessential activity (change targets). (2) It has few, if any, alternate methods of conversion. (3) It is highly dependent on fixed conditions and assumed relationships. (4) It has performers and managers who tend to focus their attention not on the *results* of the process but on the *process itself.*

It is also easier to achieve intermediate goals and objectives than long-term abstract ones. Change-resistant processes set identifiable, partial goals between initiation and ultimate accomplishment, especially when these are separated by many months or years. Wise managers devise contrived goals where intermediate ones don't exist, and link such mini-goals into a process series leading to accomplishment of the overall objective. Failing processes (processes held hostage by change) are often seen as directionless or meandering—wandering around and getting nowhere.

People simply perform better when they can see the fruits of their performance. Astute managements set achievable goals when actual ones seem beyond the reach of their workers. For the construction of a nuclear power plant, a project manager changed the yearly goal of 11 percent of overall construction of the entire plant to 100 percent of the year's work. Rather than measure net accomplishment, he chose to display the portion of the year's plan that was achieved each month. A large sign at the plant entrance proudly announced a substantial accomplishment for each month in relation to the year's goal. Workers could see *visible achievement* in terms of the yearly plan, as opposed to minute increments of the total construction effort. When milestones are too far away to see, we also should create inchstones.

Process Numbness

It's also easy to spot people responsible for or essential to the operation of a process who have been beaten down by change. They have often worked for so long with no apparent perception of accomplishment or personal contribution that the process itself becomes their only goal: the process justifies itself. Sometimes a process numbness sets in, resulting in lack of vision, rote performance, and activity that is either purposeless or is desperately seeking a justifying purpose. In a well-managed business the opposite holds true: purposes justify processes, for all successful enterprises embody processes to achieve purposes, not simply motion, not simply squirrels in a cage.

Putting the Process Down

A closer understanding of change highlights the vulnerabilities processes bring and emphasizes the need to protect our processes from any feral change we may encounter.

Every business leader is, in effect, a process manipulator. In our changing world, only the vain or the foolish overlook the prices and penalties of process management. Here are a few more:

1. No process is self-justifying, superior to purpose, permanent, independent, or isolated.

2. All processes are temporary, contrived, dependent, vulnerable to change, and subject to the laws of *expediency* as well as *efficiency*.

3. Established, continuing processes lead to *performance by rote*, dulling of expectations and experience, alienation of workers from the product of their work, insensitivity to change, undue infatuation with process (creating "process zealots"), and loss of vision.

4. The more detailed and intricate a process becomes, the more rigid, inflexible, and susceptible it becomes to damage by change.

5. The higher in value, more timeless, more abstract a *purpose* becomes, the more resistant to change its attainment will be.

6. Concentration on process activity at the expense of accomplishing results rewards *compliance*, not *creativity*.

In a World of Change, Product Enslaves Process

Because the future is certain to be racked with change, the security offered by any particular set of processes will diminish. If we like to comply with procedures, feel uncomfortable in a setting where direction is unclear, insist upon detailed compliance by our subordinates, and cannot measure anyone's performance unless with a compliance checklist of our own, we will make poor managers in change.

The managers successful in a business affected by change are those who are expedient, resourceful, and even creative—not those who are known for consistent activity; following the rules; or loyalty to the method, the cause, or even the structure of our businesses. Realizing the nature of change and the vulnerabilities any given process must entail, we will begin to value people who have the vision to see opportunities and the resourcefulness to pursue them by, when necessary, disregarding the path, the method, or the procedure useful in the past.

Strict, rote compliance will no longer be an acceptable measure of management contribution. Instead, rote compliance will become a tool needed for control of production workers, not those at supervisory or management levels.

To profit in change, then, requires that we reduce our infatuation with efficiency and begin to embrace *purpose*, *goals*, and *adaptability*. Leading thinkers in the field of manufacturing strategy seem to agree. Listen to Wickham Skinner of the Harvard Business School when describing the factory of the future (1985, p. 33):

> Manufacturing can also be a competitive weapon when it is less "efficient" but more flexible in terms of product change, in managing inevitable ups and downs in volume, in getting new products into production quickly, in providing for and consistently meeting short delivery promises, and producing with a minimum investment in inventory and fixed assets.

Fixity of purpose and efficiency of process are being dethroned as exclusive production goals. For this to be even imagined in the context of the American factory is a dramatic example of how much things have changed.

Humans and Programming

Throughout history we have been able to make any process run smoother, more consistently, and more dependably by "hard-wiring" the alternatives, decisions, and potentials inherent in the process. This means we have removed the need for judgment and room for individual impacts, as well as the fluctuations that arise because different people act differently in the same circumstances. Good process design involves programming that which may be programmed and eliminating needless decision making or interpretation. Indeed, this concept is ultimately manifested in computer programming, where machines are not allowed to "think" in any conceivable fashion but are programmed to "do," to "perform as instructed," or to "process." All the rules, routes, and actions needed are created beforehand, leaving the machine to simply perform them as told.

Process controls strive to install this same invariant performance in manufacturing systems, industrial processes, operating equipment, automobiles, and even residences. All these applications have been aided by advances in information-processing technology, especially the microchip processor. Humans write the programs and create the machines, then turn them loose together to do what has been preordained. Programs, of whatever nature, then, are embodiments of the principle described by Lewis Thomas in discussing the human body: "To do things involving practiced skills, you need to turn loose the systems of muscles and nerves responsible for each maneuver, place them on their own, and stay out of it" (1974, p. 75).

There are all sorts of programs used in the same manner, for the same reason, but having little or no relation to nerves, muscles, computers, or electronic controls. When we write a procedure for our shipping department, we are creating a program. When we create an organization and structure responsibilities within it, we are creating a program. When we give a salesperson a preferred route, series of customers, and calling quota, we are also creating a program.

Programs abound, for they are nothing more than the parameters of processes: ways to keep the activity within defined boundaries, heading in the right direction, and less subject to individual features and decisions—less "people-dependent." In fact, there are people who would like every conceivable process to be programmed, restricted, controlled, prescribed, and defined. The affected processes would then become no more than series of dominoes poised in the proper positions, simply waiting for someone to initiate their tumbling. The theory behind such programming efforts is that they reduce the incidence of unwanted change and eliminate, as far as possible, the impact of the individual. The latter is true, but the former is far from true.

People as Black Boxes

People represent the most unknown, most unanticipated ingredient in any process chain. Each person is the ultimate "black box." People represent a question mark because they are not commodities; none is identical to others. Even the same person reacts to the same stimuli differently at times, or doesn't react at all. People are not billiard balls, nor are they automatons, as much as some would have them be. When we consider change as a force in our businesses, we should consider the role of people in process functions. Do they detract from or enhance a process insofar as change vulnerability is concerned?

Conventional programming logic says that people, because of their uncertain performance and inconsistency, are anathema to any process. We would just as soon run our businesses without them. We can't assure their consistent performance.

But if we look at process design from a different perspective, people seem to rise in value, surpassing any nonvariant elements with which one might wish to replace them. For the beauty of people is their ability to think, to decide, to react to different, *nonprogrammed* conditions. This is why NASA keeps insisting on the role of astronauts in space missions. Despite the marvelous advancements made in artificial intelligence or simply in the field of computers as a whole, we still want a human aboard a spacecraft to handle nonroutine, nonprogrammable circumstances. Seen in this light, humans are our ultimate shields against the ravages of changing conditions and relationships. They make moving targets for change, unlike fixed, programmed process links. They can anticipate change, lean into it, dodge it, and quickly adapt to it once it has occurred.

It takes special people to accept the challenge of becoming astronauts and special business managers to accept the challenge of swimming in a sea of change. Every organization has such managers, but most also have their programmable counterparts—managers who are comfortable as "processors" following preestablished programs, procedures, and methods.

If we think in terms of computer programming, people in any process are comparable to multidimensional "if statements" in code. They are *logic junctions*, acting according to current conditions and the dictates of their results-oriented alignment. Seen in this manner, people become much more sensitive to change and versatile in their responses to it than if they were viewed as merely unreliable links in an otherwise hard-wired program. Programs operate by "knee jerk"; people are able to consider, to reflect, to think. When properly selected and encouraged, people become our companies' ultimate protection against change. Invariant process links are simple targets. Emphasizing product over process means we must vest our business "if statements" in people.

People within the Process

As much as people, with their innate and educated abilities to detect change and to respond intelligently, contribute to any process, they must be considered as special elements, demanding particular care and caution. While a fundamental aspect of process design calls for steps to be as small, simple, direct, and straightforward as possible ("Put this widget on this gidget"), most people resent this "bucket-brigade" logic, and it is a mistake to force it upon them. They like to think of themselves as operative, cognizant elements in a process, rather than rote performers, merely needed to receive a bucket from one person and hand it to the next.

An even greater mistake is to promote superior process performers up the organizational chain until they eventually reach a position requiring management perspective, judgment, risk analysis, and control orientations far too abstract or general for their understanding. After a certain amount of time on the bucket brigade, even the most excellent *individual contributors* lose the ability to deal with abstractions, changing objectives, shifting circumstances, and constantly redefined relationships. This makes them awful candidates for process or enterprise management. Too much time on the bucket brigade makes a person a good bucket handler but a poor manager. We must always guard against *process numbness*.

"Process": A New Management Buzzword

In recent years the notions of process design, process improvement, and even process philosophy have gained popularity and management interest. Most proponents emphasize a sharper focus on the processes our business embody and the essential elements thereof—the value each adds and the contribution each brings. This is a healthy trend not because it concerns processes per se, but because it instigates evaluation of the ability of processes to bring *results*. Process design is nothing more than results-oriented design, requiring careful consideration of product over process, elimination of noncontributing process steps (empty activity), and enhancement of those that do contribute (optimization).

A number of results-oriented trends are present in today's business communities. Most increase our awareness of change and, if followed, enhance our ability to harness domesticated change and survive the effects of unplanned versions of the phenomenon. Before examining the specific ways we can use process awareness to improve our change immunity, let's illustrate the concept.

The Click and the Stick

In the past few decades the standard ballpoint pen has been what we might call the "click" variety. Made of plastic and metal components, the click pen features a spring-loaded refillable ink tube in a modular barrel. The top of the barrel holds a device (the clicker) used to alternatively project and retract the writing point. For years this common design was taken for granted, seen in virtually every model, and accepted as a functional, results-oriented design.

For some reason, however, certain companies decided to take another look at the click pen. This look was based on the *benefits* one expects from a writing instrument as opposed to the *features* represented by it. It's not known whether this effort was termed a "process analysis" or a "results-oriented examination," but the perspective was certainly from the user's point of view. Pen makers began their examination by considering the finished product (markings on paper) and reexamining each component of the click pen (the "process" of producing those markings) in view of its essential contribution.

Looking at the production of pens from the back end (what was produced as opposed to how it was made), they eliminated a majority of the working parts of the click and came up with a much simpler, more reliable, and less expensive alternative: the "stick." The stick was bare of any noncontributing feature. No parts were designed, produced, or sold which did not directly contribute to the desired product: markings on paper. (The pen itself was correctly assumed to be merely an element of the writing process and, as such, to contain no sacrosanct parts.)

The stick is now much more popular than the click. We see it today as a simple plastic cylinder containing a fixed, nonrefillable ink barrel.

A basic plastic cap with or without an integral pocket clip protects the point, eliminating the complex and failure-prone mechanical assembly needed to project and retract the point of a click pen. Designers of the stick realized that features not bringing essential benefit are expensive, unnecessary change targets. These were tossed aside, for no features, no matter how appealing or intricate they may be, are self-justifying. The analysis that may have taken place in designing the stick pen is summarized in the table below. In this analysis, presumably, *benefits* were decided upon (what we want from a pen) and a list of the *features* of each version (what we use to achieve those benefits) was made.

Benefits	*Click features*	*Stick features*
1. Writes	1. Refill tube	1. Stick with ink
2. Protected point	Bottom barrel	2. Clip cap
3. Stays in shirt pocket	Top barrel	
4. Refillable	Screw	
	connector	
	Barrel sleeve	
	Tip cone	
	2. Tube spring	
	Tube positioner	
	Click tip	
	Barrel rifling	
	3. Shirt clip	

By choosing to market stick pens, the manufacturers reduced change targets (the wearing out of the clicker, spring, etc.) and removed nonessential dependencies on many variables that might not remain fixed, such as the supply of metal parts, the reliability of machining tools, the need to supply replacement parts and refill inserts, and the need for product assembly. Benefit-driven design is closely aligned with change-resistant design. Both improve any business process by reducing the opportunities for change to interfere with our methods of conversion. They help us add value without adding vulnerability.

Looking at Naked Purpose

Every enterprise can benefit from a fresh, tradition-independent look at the *naked purpose* for which people buy their products or services. Some have done this, with remarkable results.

A few years ago an outsider might have described the purpose of McDonald's restaurants as "making and selling hamburgers." While this was and still is a significant *activity* of that fast-food goliath, it is just that—an activity. The mission of McDonald's is not to make and sell hamburgers but to provide basic, ready-to-eat meals in a timely, clean, and efficient fashion. Taking this broader view, McDonald's decided that much more than lunchtime hamburgers was involved in fulfillment of its purpose.

Research showed a great need for, of all things, fast-food breakfasts, and McDonald's pioneered this service. Breakfast is now a considerable revenue generator, as high as 40 percent of overall revenue in some stores. And of course, the other chains have followed suit. By considering a much broader, less restricted purpose (serving the eating needs of a high percentage of society), McDonald's has escaped the traditional process restriction of the lunchtime hamburger.

People Express took a results-oriented view upon entering the commercial air transportation business. It evaluated the naked purpose of passengers and, as no surprise, determined that most simply wanted to get from point A to point B, by air, in the quickest but, most of all, least expensive manner. The established process of passenger air service had involved such nonpurposeful activities as feeding people, entertaining them, and shipping their baggage, as well as transporting their persons. People Express focused on the essential element: getting people from one place to another.

As a result, it snatched a good business from established carriers by offering price reductions—and it was able to offer the lowest prices because of, among other innovations, its stripped-down, no-frills purpose. People Express passengers were happy to pay to have their bodies hauled about the country and considered the other services extra. Some people who wanted extra services were willing to pay for them, but most people's major purpose was not to get drinks, movies, and baggage handling. Their purpose was to get to their destinations. As a result, People Express hauled a lot of warm bodies around, and, for a time at least, hauled in a lot of cash as well.

Other firms have capitalized on the notion of *process piggyback*, in which two or more purposes are tied to a single series of activities. The use of telephone directories for advertising is an example. Although telephone companies are not specifically *in* the advertising business, they can piggyback it to their activity. Now we find not only advertisements but coupons, discounts, and all sorts of promotional devices attached to our telephone directories. These devices represent a clear view of purpose-first thinking—making extra money from something one has to do anyway.

Protecting the Conversion Effect

If we want to protect conversion processes in our particular company from the vagaries of change, there are a number of ways to do so. Each relies on a knowledge of the common features and actions of change itself, and a willingness to expose everything we do to open and unprejudiced review, to results-oriented examination that takes nothing for granted and from which no sacred methods, organizations, objectives, techniques, or process steps can hide. Some of the most common ways to reduce change vulnerability are described below.

1. *Eliminate static obstacles and restraints.* Few processes can be made immune to changing conditions if they operate poorly even under static conditions. We need to begin improvements with this in mind. Most processes are deficient when they contain unnecessary steps, useless constraints, and avoidable costs. Examine each process statically to remove these before trying to install change immunity.

2. *Remove change targets.* Process steps that depend on changeable variables should be eliminated or rerouted. If we are going to assume certain conditions as fixed in order for our process to operate, let's make sure those conditions will remain fixed as the process is developed and repeated over time.

3. *Eliminate unneeded induced change or change noise.* Avoid making change for change's sake. When changes are made, make sure they are essential to the conversion process and not simply the result of tinkering with or simulation of reality. Isolate the affective essence of process change from the noncausitive noise that accompanies it (or, harking back to the analogy in Chapter 1, separate the water from the stew drippings).

4. *Allow redundancies, alternates, and parallel steps.* Unrelated steps should not be forced into a dependent situation. *Series* steps should be uncoupled and performed *in parallel* whenever possible. Each major process junction should allow consideration of alternate routes, especially if changes can frustrate us, or prevent us from taking the preferred route. A change-defiant process can swivel and pivot at many points.

5. *Superimpose results, not steps.* Whenever the same step can produce multiple results, this should be encouraged. But when two or more steps need to occur simultaneously to produce one result, this should be avoided.

6. *Consider sacrificial or disposable elements.* Few things need to last a lifetime. To "harden" a process element, in order to create endurance, is often expensive and unnecessary. Consider the lessons of "cathodic protection" and the chip watch, click pen, and disposable razor. If you have unavoidable change targets and cannot harden them, make them disposable or consumable.

7. *Encourage expediency and emphasize results.* The best process is the most expedient one, especially if it is to occur just once or a few times. Most companies penalize expediency in performance ("He didn't obey the rules," "She didn't go through channels," or "They didn't follow the procedure") and reward compliance ("She got with the program," "She doesn't make waves," "They went by the book"). This attitude must change before companies can deal with change.

8. *Allow "demonstrated abandonment."* Just as it is important to high-light and encourage change-conscious processes, it is important to pub-licly (at least within the company) discourage and discard processes that are no longer viable. We should kill obsolete processes and not simply let them fade away. Our people need to know *why* a failed process was discarded, not simply *that* it was.

9. *Ride with the tide.* Conversion processes harness change, and it is much easier to use change that is going to occur anyway, and to use it in the direction it is occurring, than to fight against it. Physical processes that harness natural forces (gravity, magnetism, entropy) are much easier to manage than those that run counter to them.

10. *Use people as they should be used.* We have all seen intelligent, cognizant people treated like on-off switches as well as program elements performing no-brain operations which machines or tools could do just as well. On the other hand, there are many situations in which needed judgment, decision-making, and extemporaneous process steps have been designed out and replaced by mechanical or rote activity. Used incor-rectly, people in a process are little more than expensive change targets. Used properly, however, they become essential contributors and valuable shields against the negative impacts of change.

Developing Contrasts

Emphasis on either processes or purposes can lead to interesting per-spectives and management activity. Some of these are shown, as they differ, in the following contrasts.

A Process Ideology Leads To:	*A Purpose Ideology Leads To:*
Commitment to technique	Independence from technique
A search for the best way	A search for many workable ways
Finding uses for our results	Finding results for our uses
Fixing hard links	Repositioning soft links
Fewer degrees of freedom	Maximum degrees of freedom
Changing the world to suit us	Changing us to suit the world
A struggle to optimize	A struggle to adapt
Questions involving "how?"	Questions involving "why?"
A premium on compliance	A premium on creativity

The Prices and Risks of Results-Driven Processes

Focusing management attention on the results of processes as opposed to their particular characteristics, on benefits rather than features, is not without potential for error or failure. Any number of misconceptions or misconstructions can occur when we start shifting emphasis toward *what is accomplished* and away from *how it is accomplished.*

As we become more results-oriented, we tend to construct more "open" processes—processes subject to interpretation, risk, and misuse. This is because the act of opening processes typically means reduction of constraints and abandonment of prescription and detailed procedures. If we are concerned about intentional abuse or circumvention, we will expose our businesses to them when our processes are less specified and when compliance is not strictly enforced. We must be judicious in allocating process freedom and in removing compliance safeguards.

In most cases, opening processes requires vesting in people and their individual judgments rather than in inanimate process steps, equipment, tools, or programs. Thus, emphasis on product over process presupposes a staff of people in whom we have confidence. It also leads to delegation of process authority to lower and lower levels and an accompanying decentralization of organizations. This is a natural effect of putting more and more decision-making responsibility in the hands of more and more people. We can't enjoy the benefits of people-dependent processes and rely on process-related human judgment while maintaining top-down pyramids of power within our companies.

It is difficult to evaluate the performance of a manager without relying on some sort of compliance checklist, rules of behavior, or performance model. Typically we measure any individual against rules (procedures, programs, activity levels, rejection rates, etc.), and the more compliance we find, the better the person's performance is judged. Shifting to results rather than process steps affects this evaluation, however. We then look not merely at how a person performs (the degree of compliance or noncompliance), but at what he or she contributes, what results ensue from the individual's efforts. This newer approach to the measure of management worth relies more on qualitative judgment, consideration of secondary and tertiary results, and long-term production as opposed to a simple reconciliation of the person with the rules. In times of change, a propensity to follow rules is not always a plus.

Managers who profit through change must be more than highly paid compliance drones, or experienced process links. They must create processes, bend them, point them in different directions.

These new leaders will be process *facilitators*, not procedure enforcers. They will point out goals, establish acceptable results, and constantly tie effort to these goals and results so that the relationship is direct and well understood throughout the organization. Everyone should know at all times both (1) what he or she is doing in relation to the conversion process and (2) the value of his or her process steps. Though specific rules and procedures are needed at the bucket-brigade level, most supervisory and management personnel will have to deal with situational rules, managing with selective latitude. To the extent that any one company's culture or leadership runs counter to these trends, it will have a difficult time converting from a process orientation to a focus on results. The companies being stranded in the world of the past are the companies whose leaders are not process facilitators but process links.

5

Slowing the March of Specialization

Winning through synthesis and adaptation

Overspecialization, say the biologists, is one of the most important contributing factors in a species' becoming extinct. When a species becomes overspecialized in a particular type of ecosystem, it is usually unable to adapt to a change in environment. It does not contain the flexibility and diversification to make the transition. The same is true with human society.

JEREMY RIFKIN

Demystification, decentralization, despecialization are the order of the day.

MARILYN FERGUSON

This chapter hits closer to personal advancement than to corporate strategy. If you think you are going to excel in changing times by becoming a specialist, you might reconsider. Specialists may *know* more about the world, or they may even *run* it. But it's the generalists who *own* it.

If companies marching on the vanguard of change were to have a banner to rally around, it would be emblazoned with the words "Syn-

76

thesize and Adapt!" More than any others, these two goals epitomize the dramatic change of direction that an appropriate response to businesschange must take. And if the static and fixed business climate of the past had had a similar banner, it would surely have read "Specialize and Optimize!"

These two phrases are much more than slogans for static and dynamic conditions. Their significance runs much deeper, to the very essence of what we call "management" and what we expect of excellent companies. In this chapter we will attempt to penetrate the symbols of these conflicting cultures and get to the heart of the attitudes and perceptions that compose the new management effort. But first, we need to recognize some specific signposts of this response to change. Most center on the trends now sweeping the landscapes of education and human relations: a slowing in the march of specialization and a renewed interest in the generalist.

Signposts of Change

- **Greater corporate interest in the liberal arts education model.** It may be hard to believe, but it's true. Although interest doesn't equate to enrollment or endowment, human resource directors are looking for the genesis of synthesis skills, and this is a possible starting point.

- **Nonmanagement positions for advanced specialists.** We cannot remain competitive if we ruin good specialists or punish those we place under them. A mistake of the past has been to promote those with narrow interests to positions requiring general concern. We must find ways to accommodate good individual contributors without forcing them into management.

- **Frequent nonfunctional job transfers.** Junior executives with high management potential will be shifted from department to department. The "grooming" that has always taken place will be structured, formalized, and open to more candidates.

- **More formal management training programs.** Increased emphasis will be on communication, dispute resolution, team building, and other synthesis skills—not simply on "how to manage."

- **More common executive job hopping.** Juniors won't be the only ones moving horizontally around the corporation.

- **More multidisciplinary teams, task forces, and projects.** Today's challenges and problems cannot be neatly confined to one or two areas of expertise. They don't recognize our organization charts.

- **Emphasis on internal communications and platform skills.** The executive in change must be an integrator and a catalyzer for mutuality.

Above all, he or she must deal with people. Writing and speaking are critical, and they are not common skills.

■ *Fewer pronounced organizational disputes.* People who draw organizational distinctions regarding credit due or boundaries overstepped will be viewed as narrow-minded or zealous. Both traits are the enemies of a change-tuned business.

■ *Increasing importance of diversity of management experience as a prerequisite to promotion.* Executives who have only done one thing, no matter for how long or how well, or at what levels, will be valued less than those who have seen other sides and performed a multitude of functions. In handling businesschange, linearity of experience is a major handicap.

Specialization: A Hangover from the Industrial Party

Specialization is the luxury and the danger of fixed conditions. It seems the longer things remain the same, the more time organisms, people, companies, and societies have to settle in, to refine themselves, and to induce internal changes that better fit them to the environment in which they operate. As they become more and more specialized, they become better and better suited to their world. Specialization, then, is nothing more than an attempt to optimize oneself under static conditions. Should all things remain constant, save for our specialization process, we would come closer and closer to perfection. Specialization under conditions of fixity is the process of becoming *better*. When things change, however, specialization is the process of becoming *obsolete*.

Just as the industrial revolution caused us to value bigger and better facilities, factories, and processes, it also required division of labor and concurrent specialization of effort to make these giant machines work at optimum levels. As more and more people became involved in any given effort, each of their respective contributions became more finite, limited, and discrete. In *The Third Wave*, Alvin Toffler quotes Prince Albert at the Crystal Palace Exhibition of 1851, when he called specialization "the moving power of civilization" (1980, p. 51). There is no better example of the legacy of the industrial revolution than the automobile assembly line, where massive capital investment is leveraged by a structured group of specialists acting in close synchronization.

As we study the difference between specialists and generalists, between the need to focus knowledge and work tasks finely or coarsely, we shall see how vulnerable specialists become to changing conditions and how the increased benefits of further specialization exact a heavy toll in change immunity. We will begin to understand that the luxury of specialized features is a liability in changing times.

What Specialization Does

When an individual or a company chooses to specialize, attention, resources, and effort are focused on a specific field or niche, and attempts are made to become better and better at exploiting that area. People, equipment, facilities, management techniques, and all other assets are valued in terms of their ability to contribute to the specialized effort. Those that contribute well are kept and nourished, while those not specifically useful are abandoned or reshaped. As time goes on, such a company (or person) becomes better and better at doing fewer and fewer things. A company may develop a specialized function (what it does, what it provides, etc.), location, methodology, or market identity, among many other features.

The lesson of specialization is that the more a company exists and operates in a certain environment (market, economy, geographic area, product field, industry, competitive posture, etc.), the more it husbands those things which facilitate its effort in that environment and the more it jettisons those things that might apply to other conditions. Specialization causes us to refine applicable features and discard inapplicable ones.

The Need to Optimize

All things being fixed, the company (person, product, etc.) that becomes best suited to its environment nudges out those less suited. The more adapted we become, the more efficient our efforts and the more we dominate the rest. This is the law of natural selection, and it applies to businesses as well as to organisms. The process of becoming more adapted and more efficient is known as "optimization."

All sorts of things can be optimized. We can attempt to achieve perfect processes, the best products, the most efficient organizational structures, the highest sales, the greatest profit, the most fail-proof procedures, the highest levels of compliance.

There are many different ways to optimize; most involve analysis, simulation, and measurement. We analyze a process by studying the conditions most favorable to its completion and by calculating the ideal ingredients, the most productive relationships, and the most reliable affective essence of the process itself. We can simulate our assumptions with computer models or by the time-honored method of trial and error (doing it again and again and seeing how it turns out—tweaking some variables, listening for the squeals of other variables, and fine tuning). And we can constantly measure results against plans, our own previous results, or the results of others in order to determine where we stand— how close to optimum we may be.

Optimization requires two analytic tools: a set of known relationships and the time needed to test and utilize them in a sequentially improving fashion. Fixed conditions foster both these tools. Change eliminates both. Change makes the knowledge of causative relationships elusive and undependable, once attained. Conditions in motion, under the effect of changes, do not allow us to repeat our work time and time again in order to refine it and its results. Change minimizes our ability to optimize. It also makes optimization a sometimes foolish pursuit.

Investing Human Capital in a Small Box

When we become more and more specialized, we not only refine our tools and equipment, but, more important, we specialize our knowledge and our skills. The more time we spend learning to be neurosurgeons, the less time and effort we have available for becoming experts in literature. Years under apprenticeship as a sculptor afford little time for obtaining an engineering degree. To the extent that knowledge gained in one field of study is transferrable or translatable to another, we reduce the exclusivity of specialization. Thus, acquiring knowledge that relates to more than one field should be a goal of anyone wanting to avoid personal obsolescence.

Investing time and talent in a special field is not unlike investing huge amounts of capital (in this case human capital) in an efficient machine or process. The more we invest, the more reluctant we are to toss aside the investment, the more chained we become to our specialty. Sometimes the chain that shackles us is made of gold and very comfortable, but it is a chain nonetheless. It prevents us from adapting easily to changed or different conditions. When we hone and redefine our skills along a special axis of knowledge, we tend to invest our human capital in one location: a very small box. And as we become better and better at that discrete skill, the box becomes smaller and smaller.

Repetition Addicts

There are other, more subtle side effects of the specialization-optimization quest. One of these involves the need to process more and more tasks pertaining to our area of expertise in order to amortize the fixed cost of it. We also have a need (not unlike the need to feed resources to a giant capital-intensive system to help pay back the initial investment) to use our skills, knowledge, and soft properties more frequently as they become more specialized—as we invest more in them. No one would willingly invest a score of years, thousands of dollars, and uncounted blood, sweat, and tears in becoming a brain surgeon only to perform one operation.

We see this tendency throughout our companies. A person who has spent 20 years in data processing positions and is transferred to the personnel department is prone to find an EDP solution to the need for more accessible employee information. A civil engineer specializing in dynamics may tend to investigate a failed building by spending an inordinate amount of time analyzing recent ground tremors or structural vibrations.

Neither of these individuals is guilty of intentional malfeasance; both are simply following personal tendencies ingrained through years of practice. They look at each problem with the best tools for observation and manipulation that they happen to possess. Because they are specialists, their best tools center on their particular specialties. Specialists become not only chained to their tools but condemned to their constant use. They become addicted to repeatability.

Building Walls and Moats

Specialized knowledge separates a person from others in terms of skill, understanding, and application biases. Specialized companies become more different from other companies as they become more and more specialized. Specialized organizational structures within a company (project teams, task forces, steering groups, committees, and the like) become more and more isolated from the general population within the company. Add to this the tendency of specialization to breed unique languages (jargon), shared experiences among the specialists, and specialized social cultures within any given company, and it becomes apparent that specialization builds walls between people and tends to separate them from each other.

One of the most difficult management tasks in a modern business is to glue specialists together in some sort of coherent, unified fashion so that all their skills can be brought to bear on a problem. Managers of specialists need to become not superspecialists but *transcenders, bridgers,* and *unifiers.* To be effective they must be excellent translators and efficient skill brokers. A major human problem with specialization, though, is that the person who is the best specialist (surgeon, engineer, accountant, reporter, teacher) is often the one placed in charge of a group of specialists—the one who most needs but, by virtue of experience, is least proficient in transcendent skills. This is when the march of specialization leads us over a cliff.

Let's Look at the Numbers

Because different specialized groups within our companies operate in terms difficult for outsiders to understand, we must measure them according to quantifiable standards. As their work changes and their results vary, the nature, character, or personality of these changes is flattened by this transposition of qualitative information to quantitative representations, and much valuable information is lost. The further a specialist group or individual grows away from management (by becoming more devoted to the speciality), the more management must rely on contrived, insensitive, and coarse management indicators. It's not that we don't trust the specialists but just that we don't understand them or their work. We must translate both into terms understandable by a layperson.

This becomes difficult to do when the specialists do not produce quantifiable results, and a good example is specialists working in research and development. Number-oriented management often has difficulty getting a handle on what R & D is doing, how close it is to a new result, or how effectively it is using invested funds. Other groups suffer from the same problem. Among these we might place public relations, personnel, data processing, and internal audit. Sometimes the ways these groups quantify their effort in order for others to understand or measure it becomes quite far-fetched and even comical.

Is This Life or Work?

Life is a general experience, involving all sorts of activity, relationships, feelings, successes, and failures. If our work is highly specialized, however, it involves relatively similar activity, specific and limited relationships, circumscribed feelings, and particular successes and failures. Because life outside work cannot become a specialized activity (except for monks or hermits), our life experiences become separated from our work experiences the more we specialize. Specialization creates another gap in this case—a gap between what we do and learn at work and what occupies the rest of our lives.

This is not to suggest that specialists are somehow stunted in their nonwork activity, but that the transfer of knowledge between what a person does in his or her specialty and outside it is hampered as the specialty become more removed and esoteric. And since life experience teaches a number of managerially significant things, specialists often miss out. Life exposes us to other people quite different from us, to circumstances less planned, to needs more general, to methods less anticipated. It prepares us for dealing with those not of our kind, in situations not of our design, with methods not of our selection. That is, in a few phrases, what management in change is all about.

The Synchronization Challenge

Each of these side effects of the march toward specialization heightens the management challenge and weakens every company when it comes to change. Changing conditions and responsibilities and shifting loyalties reinforce the need to constantly enunciate and synchronize company objectives, risks, work assignments, and methods. With a divergent group we need to more frequently establish "mental gathering points," common references and readouts about where we are and where we are going. We need to synchronize our efforts much more often than if we were managing a group of generalists, or even specialty groups during times of constant conditions.

Thinking in process terms, this means we will have a much more difficult job of programming or hard wiring a series of conversion activities. We will have to interject management influence, adding cohesive force all along the process path, not just at the beginning and end. The manager must be positioned at the pivots, where swiveling and flexing occur in response to change. The manager can no longer afford to simply plan work and measure the outcome. The manager must be the glue holding the work together, the bandleader ensuring that everyone is playing the same tune, note by note.

The Upsetting Nature of Change

By eliminating fixity of condition and disrupting cause-effect relationships, change makes specialization questionable and causes us to reevaluate the need for optimization. As we become better and better at any one conversion process or business effort, we simultaneously reduce our ability to adapt rapidly to changing conditions. Specialization makes us dependent on fixed conditions and vulnerable to changing ones. We become more *adapted* but less *adaptive*.

If economies of scale and constant trial and error are two of the most productive tools of optimization, they become unattainable or unworkable when dynamic differences begin to occur. It's impossible to establish relationships and to exploit them time and again when the very foundations upon which they rest are constantly shifting. Changing conditions make flexibility and adaptability more important features of any person, process, or business enterprise. This means that, in light of change, we need to revise our notion of *optimum* itself.

In its broadest sense, the term "optimum" can no longer be used as a synonym for "efficiency" or "adaptation." Simply because something is productive, useful, and ideally adapted to any given setting is not reason enough to consider it optimum, to consider it the best we can achieve. We need resources, skills, and managements that are as adapted as possible to current conditions yet never so well adapted that they cannot react properly to changing ones. Whenever specialization causes the abandonment of *adaptive* skills or features at the expense of *adapted* ones, it exacts a price. That price is a reduction in change immunity. We are most immune to change when we are best able to transcend conditions and continue to perform at acceptable, not necessarily optimum, levels.

Change causes us to reconsider the advisability of refinement. In light of the upsetting nature of induced change, managements must constantly contrast its added benefit by weighing incremental value thus gained against any restrictions it places upon us. There is always some point along the optimization-specialization path at which increased adaptation carries too high a price. To profit in changing times we must move just up to that point but no further; we must exploit adaptation without becoming exploited by it.

Changing Premiums

The phenomenon of change upsets many of our static-based perspectives and forces us to value certain characteristics more or less than we would under fixed conditions. Change puts a premium on the ability of a person or company to shift, to pivot, and to adapt new and more relevant abilities, methods, and outlooks. All these tend to reduce the value of specialization, whether in our personal knowledge, in company processes, or in management scaffolding.

Change removes the need to achieve consistent and repeatable results, creates diversity, and causes business leaders to look at qualitative indicators of success rather than simply at quantitative representations. This is because adaptability to potential conditions is so difficult to ascertain or to measure. We have no proven way of comparing losses in present efficiency with gains in change immunity. We must rely on human judgment and qualitative management values. We cannot simply look at the numbers, because the numbers always point in the direction of specialization and continued refinement of what it is we are, or are doing, at the present time, under the present conditions.

Optimization requires a business and its managers to place high premiums on the ability to *use* something as extensively as it can be used. Adaptability, on the other hand, causes us to value our ability to create, to assimilate, to *synthesize* as quickly as we can. This ability has long been the forte of the generalist, not the specialist. Listen to Toffler: "Our job here will be to think like generalists, not specialists" (1980, p. 130).

The Strengths of Generalization

If generalized businesses and their managements are unable to fully exploit fixed conditions, as most are, they make up for this apparent weakness by being able to quickly respond to changing conditions. Rapid detection, understanding, and harnessing of new situations and new tools is a practice every company should value highly. It requires general knowledge, broad management concepts, and widely focused management vision. Today's successful manager must be able to synthesize resources and forces, to bring together differing skills and quickly focus them on more fleeting opportunities.

This all points in the direction of generalization. Generalists themselves are more adaptable, more expedient, and more malleable. They flex and bend in the wake of change, reorient themselves and their companies, and continue to pursue whatever goals they have established without much disruption. In order to quickly synthesize diverse organizations, skills, and resources, generalists must deal in common languages, transcending the walls and gaps between them. Here again, generalists provide the cohesive force to bind disparate efforts and the vision to point them in a common direction.

Generalists bring no intrinsic value to any business effort beyond their ability to synthesize and to manage the specialty efforts of others. Their focus is the whole, not the separate parts. Their interest is on environments and outcomes, not so much on particular techniques or methods. They never become loyal to any given set of circumstances or to any management tool or conversion process, but constantly scan the horizon for new needs, new tools, and new, more adaptive syntheses.

One can't help but suspect that broad-minded generalists must have been at work when American Express decided to expand from a narrow-scope credit card firm to a giant in the financial services field. Specialists would have said something like "Let's become a damned good credit card concern, let's optimize what we do now." The result would have been to condemn the company to the past. Instead, someone must have said, "We're in the financial services business anyway, let's take advantage of what we've got."

We all know the result. American Express is now a full-service lender, travel services firm, insurer, and provider of many other related services. It is much more than a good credit card firm; it is a financial titan, in large measure because of its generalists, we must presume. And it didn't need to diversify, to buy into vastly different industries, or to take other management risks normally associated with growth. It simply generalized what it did best.

U-Haul Corporation followed the same logic when it converted from a specialty rental outfit to a more general services company. It spread out sideways (generalized) by piggybacking small package delivery, warehousing, and tool rental to existing operations. With minor additional investment, few or no new skills required, and therefore little incremental risk, the company parlayed a narrow-scope function into a broader one. Its generalization took a form mentioned above. That is, U-Haul looked at its *naked purposes* (the renting and moving of vehicles) and enhanced each associated process. It now has several revenue generators instead of one, all achieved with minor internal change or added exposure. That's what generalization is all about.

Slowing the March

If one accepts the value of generalization in view of the effects of change, the next questions asked must be "Why are we so short of effective generalists?" and, perhaps, "Why can't successful specialists 'adapt' to this need and become more generalized?" The answer to both concerns the way in which we select, train, and nurture our people. In any field of expertise or business a number of factors reinforce and promote specialization and punish or stunt a desire to generalize. The unfortunate result is that "most people are culturally more skilled as analysts than synthesists" (Toffler, 1980, p. 130).

Take the initial hiring of any new employee. Seldom do we seek to employ an "apprentice generalist." More often we are looking for a particular type of person, with special skills, for placement in a particular process link. We hire workers, at all levels of salary and position, to fit specific needs and to perform accordingly. We restrict our view to those who fit the mold we have in our minds, to fit the needs of a specific vacancy. We hire specialists.

Knowing this, most students focus their education in specific directions, with the hopes of gaining specific skills and making themselves employable, sought after, wanted. They know that companies do not hire people with degrees in *synthesis, assimilation*, or *transcendence*, but in accounting, engineering, chemistry, and law. Quite naturally, all of these aspiring students would like to rise within their eventual companies to positions which challenge their generalized skills and broad potentials, but they realize that they'll never reach those positions unless they enter the company through a narrow doorway: specialization.

Another factor causes us to continue to use specialists as such even though they may be ripe for movement to more expansive challenges. A good accountant is sometimes seen as so valuable as an accountant that we cannot afford to lose that capability by promoting him or her to company treasurer. An experienced mechanical engineer is seen as necessary to field operations of a construction contractor, and so cannot be brought back to the home office to gain exposure to marketing, finance, personnel, or project management.

Of course, there are some enlightened companies that realize the need, and can afford, to cross-train employees in order to groom them for more generalized responsibilities, but these are few and the selection processes they use are often governed by favoritism, serendipity, or simply "good timing." In the end, and for most businesses, a *good specialist* is often doomed to a life as a *permanent specialist*. And the longer a person is used as a specialist, the more difficult eventual transcendence to generalized perspectives becomes. The longer you dig in the trenches, the deeper you get and the more difficult it is to jump out.

Our Own Worst Enemies

People in the business community who wish greater responsibility, broader challenge, and more generalized experiences (in other words, those who aspire to executive positions) often are their own worst enemies in this quest. Many of us seem to cling to the comfort specialization offers without realizing the danger it presents. We may be reluctant to discard the benefits of specialization because (1) it makes us unique, (2) it adds to our present value, (3) it causes us to consider ourselves irreplaceable, (4) it makes us special and distinct from all the rest (giving us a valuable identity), and (5) generalization tends to increase our dependence on others.

This notion of dependency on others leads us to consider the different ways these two kinds of people, specialists and generalists, succeed in a modern business climate. Whether outstanding engineers, teachers, welders, disc jockeys, or surgeons, specialists constantly seek optimal solutions—the best ways of doing what they do best. Generalists, on the other hand, often search for pragmatic, expedient solutions. Specialists strive for accuracy, while their generalist counterparts place a higher value on workability. Whereas specialists often work with things (accountants with balance sheets, engineers with equations, lawyers with the intricacies of legal briefs), generalists most often work with people.

A process focus is most common among specialists, while a focus on outcomes, regardless of how they were attained, is seen among generalists. Specialists work with immutable or at least temporarily fixed laws and relationships (the law of gravity, generally accepted accounting principles, the constitution of the United States), and generalists work with situational rules and relationships. In the end, most specialists succeed individually or in small groups, while most generalists succeed through the efforts of others. Considering all these differences and remembering the upsetting influence of change, it's not difficult to understand why individual contributors to any business effort (specialists) often make poor managers.

A Need for Both Specialists and Generalists

We need specialists and special processes to succeed in any given business environment, and we need generalists and generalized processes to succeed in changing environments. We cannot do without one or the other; we need both. The "optimum" combination, therefore, allows specialized skills to operate while they can and as best they can, while others (generalists) oversee their work, synthesize it with the work of others, and constantly peer over the horizon to determine whether realignment is needed.

An understanding of the strengths and weaknesses of each approach helps us strengthen both and adapt them to change. The process of acquiring this understanding emphasizes "where we are going" and "why we are going there" for each group, and puts less value on "who" or "how" for both. Businesses that operate well in change define themselves and their people by results and not by action, by "what I did" rather than by "what I am." In an ever-changing, results-oriented environment, results and action become the same.

Developing Contrasts

People tend to view the world differently depending on whether their mental sets are of a specialist or a generalist cast. In order to further define the differences between specialization and the more change-responsive generalism described here, we can contrast these two different, often opposing views.

A Specialized View Sees:	*A Generalized View Sees:*
A whole to be divided into components	Components to be assimilated into a whole
The dimension of depth	The dimension of breadth
Exclusive postures and intentions	Mutual concerns and interests
Deduced principles	Induced concepts
An accurate view of one scene	A representative view of many scenes
A need to perfect adaptation	A need to improve adaptability
Value in being a sole expert	Value in using many experts
The benefits of investing in a skill	The benefits of investing in many awarenesses
Applications chasing opportunity	Opportunity waiting for application

The Prices and Risks of a New Premium on Synthesis

Although we have described several reasons for slowing the march of specialization among ourselves, our conversion processes, and our companies, the pursuit of adaptability is not without prices and risks that need addressing. If it is true that "we stand on the edge of a new age of synthesis," as Toffler suggests (1980, p. 130), most of us, together with our companies, may find entrance to that age a bit painful.

The first price generalization extracts is the inability to optimize. Because change causes us to restrain optimization or at least to proceed very deliberately and carefully down its path, there is a chance that no affective change will occur and we will miss the opportunity to become efficient. If our competitors take the optimization risk, they may become more efficient and more adapted, and thus may nudge us out of the environment. Thus an eye toward the potential of change sometimes causes us to miss incremental exploitation. Not only will it cause pursued opportunities to be underdeveloped, but it will also tend to keep us away from unpursued but profitable ones. If we think a trend will last only a few months and instead it continues for years, we will have missed the chance to capitalize on it entirely.

Granted that each management group needs synthesizers, assimilators, or generalists, the cost of obtaining and maintaining these is sometimes high. It requires careful selection, training, and exposure of certain individuals in order to nurture general perspectives among them. This means that they will often be underutilized or not utilized productively at all. If we measure company divisions by looking strictly at the short-term bottom line, the cost of this nurturing may be deemed too high. Nurturing general abilities is the same as nurturing potential; it returns nothing until used. Even though the existence of general abilities is a net positive for the company, they may represent a negative for the group housing them. It is also much more difficult to assess the contribution or performance of generalists than of specialists who operate with testable skills to produce measurable results.

None of these comments should be construed as a denigration of the value or personality of any given group of specialists, of any profession or skill. On the contrary, regardless of our response to or ignorance of change, we will always need special skills, distinct disciplines, and finely focused perspectives. But only by realizing the ways their perspectives differ from those of a more general nature can we begin to better assimilate specialists into the fabric of company management.

A reluctance to adapt because it might make us less adaptive when change occurs is much like an unwillingness to spend money today because it may cause our reserves for future use to dwindle. Taken to extreme, however, potential brings no value unless it is ultimately used. Stashing money away in the mattress for a rainy day is sometimes prudent, but if all we have is so placed, we end up in poverty today— impoverished by our potential. Poverty to an individual is similar to bankruptcy for a company. If we can't turn a profit on today's work simply because we are afraid the situation may change, it will in fact change: we will dissolve. Prudent investment in today's opportunities without undue depletion of tomorrow's potential is the challenge of change. No company can exist with only well-developed conjecture and well-guarded potential. Someone has to pay the bills today.

Just as we need specialists and generalists, we need people who can focus on the finer details of our present business as well as people who can focus on the larger picture and on the upcoming future. The best combination in any one person, though, is the ability to quickly change this focus, from close up to far away and back again at will. The manager who resembles a variably focused camera lens is the manager best adapted to a changing world—most adaptive, best able to ride the waves of change without being overwhelmed by them.

6

Investing in Human Capital

Harvesting the potential of people

But what man will do to himself he doesn't really know. A certain scale of time and a ghostly intangible thing called change are ticking in him.

LOREN EISELEY

We must now confront an almost inevitable conclusion: people are critical to our ability to detect, adjust, and respond to change. To profit in change we must profit through people. A chorus of trends leads us to admit this particular dependence on the human factor in the business equation, and to underscore the growing role of *human capital* as each commercial enterprise strives for change immunity.

In light of what is known about the action and effects of change, we simply cannot continue to treat people as merely another type of business resource, as another variable among many in the managerial mix of relationships. They demand much more of us, and because of the special features they offer, they bring us more. Any company wishing to do more than just survive change—to cohabit with it and even to thrive under its actions—must nurture and develop its human capital.

The value each company places on human capital varies with the role of humans in its conversion process; the level of managers and professionals as opposed to production workers; and the influence of outside factors such as unions, professional associations, and the business culture itself. Because of this, each company will respond differently to the need to develop human capital, and will respond to a greater or lesser extent than that suggested here. What is certain, however, is that all companies must focus management attention on the human element, no matter how it has been treated in the past, and must enhance their understanding of the role and power humans offer in view of change. Sometimes this leads to specific changes and special emphasis, such as the ones listed here.

Signposts of Change

- *Larger training budgets and programs.*   More money is going into people, and more management attention is being directed at how much good it does.

- *More outside seminars, workshops, symposiums.*   Just look at your daily mail. Anyone not receiving at least five seminar flyers a week should feel offended.

- *Wider, less uniform salary and benefit ranges.*   People are being treated as individuals, not commodities. Salaries are ways to pay for today's work but also for the potentials or promises of tomorrow.

- *Fewer automatic, insensitive transfers and reassignments.*   The human impacts of relocation are so great that the way it is done must not be insensitive. Company loyalty is nonexistent; people are loyal to themselves and their careers. Good people don't have to move—and they don't move unless they want to.

- *Mandatory continuing education policies.*   Many professions now enforce these. Many companies will soon do so. Knowledge is moving and changing. We can't expect what we learned years ago to suffice.

- *Emphasis in recruiting on growth, culture, and lifestyle in addition to salary and function.*   The valued candidate wants a nurturing climate, not an extractive one.

- *More cross-functional orientation, awareness training, and exposure opportunities.*   People are demanding the chance to learn about all sides of the operation and the company. They know their particular side or their particular slot might disappear, and they want to protect themselves against this eventuality.

■ *Broader dissemination of company information.* In our information-based world, depriving a person of information is the social equivalent of locking him or her in the company closet. People who are told, "You don't need to know" hear "You don't need to exist."

The Inevitable Conclusion

A number of factors presented in previous chapters point to human beings as the chief defense against the damages of change. First, as we have seen, the heavy costs and incremental penalties of a high dependence on fixed capital (the so-called hard properties of physical plant, equipment, machinery, and the like) cause us to reduce this type of investment. And because people are excellent change shields, pivoting and flexing in the wake or in anticipation of change, it makes sense to invest in these capabilities as an alternative.

If slowing the march of specialization affords more change resistance, human investment generates dividends in this regard also. Taken as a whole, human beings can become more generalized than our other assets, and at a quicker pace. It is difficult to imagine a manufacturing line switching from producing automobile tires to making lipstick at a moment's notice, but a flexible, adaptive manager should be able to make this shift fairly quickly, transferring those talents, skills, and methods that transcend the product differences almost at will. Even though specialized education and use tend to cast them in specialty molds, people demonstrate remarkable abilities to adapt to more general responsibilities once given the chance. Machines have much more trouble making such a transition.

Although there are many who cling to processes, or hide behind them, most mature managers are independent of specific methods of conversion. This lack of process dependency makes people much more expedient users of resources and much more results-oriented than hard-wired, programmed properties. People are, as already mentioned, the best "if statements" we can use. They can respond or react along a multitude of dimensions once change is impending or occurring. Even the best computer programs or situationally responsive procedures must react according to a limited number of preordained choices. Unlike programmed assets, people can be extemporaneous, imaginative, and spontaneous.

As much as they annoy us, as difficult as they are to measure, quantify, and control, and as unpredictable and nonuniform as they are, people remain the only repositories of human capital. It is in them, and in them alone, that we must vest so much of the planning, performing, and control essential to business management. In times of fixed conditions and steady-state relationships, we could afford to denigrate the variable nature of people and diminish those qualities responsive to change. We could treat people as essential nuisances or as workers for which a more cost-beneficial machine had yet to be developed. The days when those conditions and relationships existed, if they ever did exist, are certainly gone.

People—with their wonderfully adaptive capabilities, their powerful analytic and intuitive skills, and their irreplaceable creativity—are our most precious and most demanding resources. They come to us by various routes, mostly by serendipity, already full of valuable attitudes, approaches, skills, and abilities—full of *embedded capital.* If we are to manage in change, we must manage with our human resources, and we must develop and nurture the capital they bring and their unique potential, among all other resources, to generate more for us. We must develop human capital.

Two Types of Business Capital

If we think of business capital as that which our company retains and which brings value to us, we can classify it as either *attached* or *embedded.* Attached capital is made up of both hard and soft properties, and includes such things as physical plant, equipment, proprietary methods, and inventory. Embedded capital, on the other hand, is more difficult to identify. It can best be described as that which, although often intangible and immeasurable, nonetheless contributes value to our company. In this category we would, of course, include our people, but we could also include our business reputation, our company culture, and our *invisible potential,* that which we have the capability of becoming but have not yet become.

This final feature is never shown on the balance sheets, never measured, and almost impossible to quantify. Nevertheless, companies that are entirely viable and very successful at what they are presently doing must be valued lower than those of a similar type having potential to become even larger, better, and more change-resistant in the future.

For example, the assets of a farmer at the end of a harvest period can be divided into these two categories. The attached capital might include planting and cultivating equipment, fertilizer, the land itself, and the corn harvested at the end of the growing season. The present value of all these can be seen, touched, and measured. What remains are the farmer's knowledge, skills, and willingness to plant another crop, as well as the seeds held back as potential for the future. These seeds are the farm's embedded capital, and simply because we cannot easily quantify its value is no reason for it to be discounted or ignored. In this example, in fact, embedded capital is often more valuable, less replaceable, and more essential than that which is attached.

It is this potential, this future capability, which allows the farmer to continue to operate successfully. Without it the attached capital—the tractors, cultivators, sprayers, barns, silos, and even land itself—will sooner or later rust, decompose, degenerate, and grow fallow. Embedded capital is essential not only because it allows the leveraging of attached capital at any given time but also because it holds the promise of tomorrow. Without this promise every farm and every farmer become little more than temporary phenomena: consumable items. The same can be said for all other businesses.

In this regard the company that looks only at today's marketable assets, today's values, is not unlike the unwise farmer who consumes all his own grain, neglecting to set some aside for seed. He thus exploits the present worth at the expense of its future potential, seeing only the attached capital it represents and missing the embedded capital it promises. Many shortsighted companies do the same. These fail to invest in the human capital they will so desperately need to survive in a changed world. Because they cannot see, measure, or extract immediate profit therefrom, they discount or ignore the many generations of crops these figurative "seeds" represent. They eat their own seeds.

Understanding Attached and Embedded Capital

The point of distinguishing between attached and embedded capital is to broaden our understanding of the special features of people, for they alone add value to or represent most of our business potential, especially when we consider the effects of change. People are the center of embedded capital. Only by understanding the sharp and muted distinctions between these two types of assets can we develop a mature, change-conscious appreciation for the need to develop and nourish human capital.

Attached capital, as mentioned above, is fairly easy to identify. It is externally visible; we know when it exists and where it is at any given time, and we can usually quantify it, measure its costs and contributions, and judge its value. Embedded capital is not so easily seen or quantified. We often know of its presence (or absence) only through its actions or inactions, only through its tracks. As such, embedded capital is seldom "seen." Rather than visible, it is *demonstrable*.

Attached capital is generally situationally insensitive. That is, it cannot move, adapt, or act in accordance with changes in condition or circumstance. Consider the farmer's tractor, for example. It remains the same regardless of whether (1) the weather changes, (2) the type of crop planted varies, (3) the farmer uses it frequently or less so, (4) other tractors or substitutes are developed and made available, or (5) its economic viability increases or diminishes.

Considering the farmer's willingness to continue farming as an example of embedded capital, we know it will change in response to all these factors and many more. As conditions change in the product marketplace (grain market), as prices vary in the farming mix, and as the farmer's perception of the nonquantifiable values associated with farming (business independence, self-sufficiency, closeness to nature, intimacy with family, and so forth) vary, his willingess to continue farming changes. Embedded capital is situationally sensitive.

Not only is embedded capital situationally sensitive, it is also more situationally independent than any attached versions. It can change without external stimuli, and it can modify itself according to its own demands and expectations. Fixed, attached assets have no such freedom. They remain tied to the situation and uses to which they are applied. They are situationally dependent. Like the machines strung along a highly efficient manufacturing line, they depend upon the continuation of a specific, highly regulated process. Once the process stops or is significantly modified, the value of the attached capital diminishes rapidly. The result is that attached capital is more fixed and embedded capital is more variable.

Attached capital is easily eroded, and the pace of the erosion is often connected with use or time's passage. Equipment wears out, breaks down, or becomes obsolete by newer, more efficient models or alternative processes. Embedded capital, on the other hand, is not so vulnerable. Being ingrained rather than existing on surfaces, it often remains buried and protected—below the surface where erosion cannot reduce its value.

Here we can make a significant distinction between specialized, lower-level conversion *skills* and more general, higher-level *approaches*. While both can be considered soft properties, even human capital, the former is much more like attached capital in that it is often situationally dependent (pertaining to a specific process, for example) and can degenerate over time. Approaches, and more precisely those approaches pertaining to management objectives, tend to resist changes to any given set of conditions and to survive for long periods of time. If we think of management talents as comparable with product features, then, skills are less change-resistant than properly founded approaches. Approaches offer a higher level of change resistance than skills, just as symbols projected by a product are more immune than the product itself.

Most assets improve by becoming better attuned to current conditions and expectations, by becoming specialized. Whether manifested as machinery, information systems, or company procedures, attached capital needs to be specialized to improve. Embedded capital, on the other hand, is often made more valuable as it is generalized. The more general it becomes, the more adaptive to future needs it will be; and the future is when embedded capital will pay dividends. If embedded capital can be stylized as *potential*, then general potential is much more precious than specialized potential in a world that is changing.

Finally, we must admit that although machines, for example, tend to decompose through repetitive uses, human capital tends to *atrophy with disuse*. An automobile with fewer miles on the odometer is more valuable than one with excessive mileage, one that has been driven a great deal. A manager who has made fewer decisions in the course of a career, though, is often less valuable than a manager whose figurative "decision odometer" has been turned over once or twice.

With extended use, embedded capital grows, unfolds, and regenerates, while attached capital erodes, wears, and declines in value. The more we use machines, the less they are able to be used, but the less we use people's embedded potential, the less it is able to be used. This is a key principle in any quest for the development of greater human capital. Human capital cannot be protected or improved by simply not making use of it often. It is much like grandma's pristine car in that it needs to be taken out for a spin every so often whether we need to go somewhere in it or not. Otherwise atrophy sets in—and atrophy, like nonrecognition, is one of the worst enemies of human capital.

Human judgment, intuition, or even "gut feel" cannot and should not be programmed out of those who must respond to changing conditions. As Wickham Skinner emphasizes, "The fantastic abilities of people to plan, remember and use judgment, wisdom, and intelligence extend far beyond the capabilities of computers and automation. Therefore, economics often favors the use of people" (1985, p. 34).

Human Capital: The Miracle Worker

The relative significance of attached and embedded capital has been clearly demonstrated in situations where one or the other has been destroyed. A case in point has been the "miraculous" rebirth of the economies of Japan and western Europe, particularly West Germany, from the ashes and rubble of World War II. Both countries went from ragged industrial basket cases to modern, efficient world economic powers in just a few years. Most of this growth has been attributed to attached capital, such as the massive doses of economic aid given under the Marshall Plan and similar programs. New factories, housing, transportation, and communication networks quickly sprang up amid the ruins of a destroyed infrastructure, and each nation quickly resumed world-class standing. Was this miracle of reindustrialization strictly caused by the infusion of attached capital, or were other forces responsible?

Some suggest that although capital formation was essential, it was not *responsible* for the ensuing economic phenomenon. They point out that a similar program of capital formation would have failed in most any other underdeveloped country, even today, because of what all the bombs, fires, and deprivation of World War II failed to destroy—the human capital of Germany and Japan. Though the buildings, plants, roads, and railways (the physical infrastructure) may have been destroyed, the embedded capital (the social and human infrastructure) survived.

This embedded capital consisted of the highly educated population—doctors, engineers, accountants, teachers, scientists—and the working middle class—farmers, tradespeople, clerks, and civil servants. Also remaining were the social and cultural networks holding these civilizations together: the institutions promoting and controlling joint effort, the trade associations, professional societies, commercial organizations, educational institutions, social clubs, charities, and industry groups. These networks make up the fabric of any society, and without them no amount of attached capital will help. Although the fabric of these two countries might have been rent by the war, the pattern and knowledge needed to repair it remained intact. Human capital can repair or replace attached capital. The converse has yet to be seen.

Even today, we see political manifestations of this same principle. One is the persistence of the U.S.S.R., despite international scorn, in opposing the emigration of Jews to Israel. Soviet officials maintain this policy not on ideological grounds or for purposes of national pride. They simply want to prevent the drain of educated, motivated, and contributing members from their society. They want to keep a valuable asset, an irreplaceable one, from running out on them—even if this requires force and invites universal condemnation.

Human capital is thus considered so important that it must be kept at all costs, even in chains. The lesson of postwar Japan and Germany, however, is that wonderful achievements are possible when human capital is set free.

Two Business Cultures:
Extractive and Nurturing

The way a company views and treats its embedded capital often indicates whether the company will survive change. Two extremes exist: *extractive cultures*, or those companies that see human capital as a resource to be exploited today, and *nurturing cultures*, or those that place a higher value on the potential of human capital.

Extractive industries are those which find untapped resources, such as iron ore, gold veins or coal seams, and take them from nature for fairly immediate use by society. Extraction is often considered exploitation; material is taken with little or no investment in it, is simply moved from point of discovery to point of use. In extraction we need not develop the material, create conditions fostering its growth, feed it, or otherwise invest in its being. We simply find it and take it.

Nurturing industries, of which farming is the most common example, must invest in their products before they can exploit them. A farmer must secure land, till the soil, plant seed, fertilize, guard against pests and weeds, and hope for favorable weather until such time as harvesting is possible. A true nurturing industry, agriculture is based on the ability to foster, direct, and facilitate growth. We seldom find and use agricultural products; we must develop them, nurture them, and coax the changes we desire. Only after this commitment and investment are made can we expect to reap the benefits of our risk and our labor. And once each harvest is complete, we must take steps—soil protection, seed isolation and storage, and crop rotation—to assure that future harvests using the same potential will be possible.

In extractive industries none of these steps are necessary. We cannot grow iron ore, nor create conditions assuring its reappearance. We can only move on to unexploited territory and look for iron as it exists in its natural state, waiting for us to "take" it.

There are companies that follow the extractive model with regard to human capital. These companies value people only as they exist in their encountered state and look for the best ways to "use" them. Although a use orientation is also present with companies following the alternative model—nurturing—it is predicated on development and enhancement of naturally occurring capital rather than on the mere taking of what's there to begin with. Extractive companies, regardless of their goods or services, are therefore directed by depletion, while nurturing companies are directed by human growth. Seen in this light, it becomes fairly obvious which group is better equipped for the changes that are upon us.

Depletion or Growth

Depletion-directed companies have no need for skills or methods that help create human potential, because they use only that potential created elsewhere—that potential brought to them by their employees. Companies operating in a culture focused on nurturing, however, see a need or have a desire to create potential themselves, developing it in their employees before expecting to harvest it. They realize that management potential and management perspectives, like perishable products, have a very short shelf life, that they should be used almost immediately and must have constant care. Extractors, on the other hand, often view the same management potential and management perspectives as fixed, nonperishable, and inert, like buried ore, waiting unchanged until needed and mined.

Whereas mineral products (oil, coal, iron, cooper, etc.) degrade with use, causing extractive industries to move on in search of new sources, renewable products and their potential are often enhanced by use. The same is true if we extend the comparison to companies extracting management talent and those nurturing it. Extractive companies use what's there and discard what remains, while nurturing companies are constantly working to rejuvenate, enhance, and develop what exists so that it may yield many harvests into the future.

Besides the shortsightedness of applying extractive philosophies to human resources, another problem is that it fails to appreciate the multifaceted nature of human capital. While a mineral commonly exists in one physical state (solid or gaseous, for instance), human capital exists in many different states, at many different levels of value, each of which changes over time. Iron ore doesn't get any more concentrated or rich as time goes on, but management attitudes, perceptions, and confidence can either improve or degrade with time. What companies do during that time, how they treat human capital, has a major bearing on its usefulness and, indeed, on its value.

Aside from government-ordered reclamation efforts, extraction of mineral ore requires no investment in it or in its surroundings. We simply take and go, cut and run. To nurture potential, in contrast, requires continuing investment; we must reimburse the repositories of human capital before and during the harvest process. We cannot cut and run, at least not more than once. While extractive companies move on to other people once they have exploited those at hand, nurturing companies must regenerate their resources not only after harvesting but before depletion occurs.

Extractive and nurturing industries (mining and farming) have been compared here in order to cast some light on their figurative counterparts among business enterprises. Without question there are many companies that, either expressly or through their actions, treat human beings among their management ranks as merely so much iron ore waiting to be used, with little investment and no thought of regeneration, development, or cultivation. More enlightened companies take the opposite approach, fostering a nurturing culture which places higher value on management potential than on immediate exploitation of today's talents. Obviously, keeping their potential well developed, well fed, and well appreciated makes nurturing companies much better equipped to face changing conditions. Extractive companies do not nourish that which doesn't give immediate payback. They face change as do farmers who eat their seeds: they consume their potential and thereby consume themselves.

Ways to Develop Human Capital

In developing human capital, it's not enough to merely recognize the wide disparity between extractive and nurturing philosophies. Much more is needed beyond recognition of the important role people play in the managerial mix. Nurturing companies benefit not from what they espouse but from what they do. Talk and images never yield a harvest. Work, investment, and commitment are necessary. A company wishing to protect itself from the vagaries of change by nurturing its people—its powerful change defense—needs to understand and implement these specific policies:

1. *Broaden the selection process.* A broader selection process is needed when seeking management candidates: a process that recognizes and values potential as well as existing strengths in each individual. Companies often fill their management staffs with people who stumble upon the company through serendipity or who just happen to be available. No farmer would sow his fields with the seeds that nature brings in by way of the wind or animal carriers; a crop of weeds would result. We must change our selection criteria by adopting an approach sensitive not only to the grain we can make of each seed today but to the plants that each seed represents for tomorrow.

2. *Promote general exposure.* With generalists being potential change shields and representing our potential for transcending changed conditions unscathed, we must take steps which result in constant general exposure of our managements—exposure that will pay dividends dif-

ficult to measure and relate, but dividends nonetheless. Exposing managers to different perspectives, different approaches, and tangential processes is often affected by change float itself, for exactly when and how results will surface is a matter of hopeful speculation. We cannot insist on directly proportionate and immediately usable benefits. If these were our only criteria we would keep specialists in their special boxes, never to peer outside—never to generalize.

3. *Increase information beyond subsistence.* A premise of Malthusian economics is that workers should be kept, or will tend to be kept, at subsistence wages, with company owners doling out only so much as is necessary to keep them alive and thereby assure their return to work each day. Modern company executives have taken this notion to the field of information, and the result is that they keep their managements on information diets at subsistence levels—telling them only what they "need to know." This is not the way to broaden their perspective, to create the generalists needed for change immunity, or to nurture management potential. An organism fed only what it needs to *survive* does not get the extra nutrition necessary to *grow*.

4. *Let development cascade downward.* A nurturing culture perpetuates itself by insisting that each level of management nurture the levels below it. Managers are judged not only by their production of quantitative value (profit and loss) but by their development of potential. This should be promoted and guarded, and any measurements of a manager's worth should take this element into account.

5. *Allow discretionary management.* No matter what we pay managers, nor how full and extensive their perks become, those worth keeping will resist being treated with suspicion, delegated responsibility without authority, or assigned to prolonged duty on the company bucket brigade. Managers should be treated not as highly paid process links but as valued people in whom we have placed the process itself. We must defer to their discretion from time to time and must give them room to act on their individual judgment, for judgment is a perishable item and soon atrophies if not used. It needs to be driven around the block once in a while.

6. *Identify and reward creativity.* As our ultimate "if statements," people, and especially managers, should have the freedom to create the conditions and processes they need, rather than being required simply to comply with those created by others. Creativity and imagination are two examples of perishable embedded capital. They are also essential to the ability to adapt to changing conditions. The higher an individual climbs within the company and the more the company is exposed to

change, the more important it is to nourish that individual's creativity and imagination.

7. *Share exploration of alternatives.* No manager has potential if he or she doesn't value it. While many company cultures denigrate people's desire for advancement, for generalization, and for higher levels of business consciousness—"He's too aggressive"; "She's thinking of her own future"; "They should stick to their own business"—these features should be treated as meritable in view of the action of change. We need to continuously define short- and long-term career paths, alternatives, and potential for every valued manager. We must always look to the future with our managers, and make sure they see us looking.

8. *Identify contributions and accomplishments.* Every person works better and develops skill faster when able to see the fruits of his or her labor. There is no manager more lost and hopeless than the one who cannot detect his or her individual contribution to the company effort and results thereof. Simply performing an ordered function does not provide enough feedback on results to keep a valued manager satisfied. While this may work for apprentices or production labor, it is far short of the expectation of today's manager. Whether natural or contrived, final or intermediate, the span between activity and results should be as short as possible in order to satisfy managers' need to see the fruits of their labor.

And when a specific task is completed, or a goal is achieved, people need to pause and *celebrate*. Managers are no different from production workers in this regard. They enjoy seeing a job well done. Unfortunately, many jobs tend to fade out as they approach completion, and to end with a whimper. We should strive to avoid this; each task or assignment should finish with a bang, one that can be heard by the responsible managers. Analogous to feedback on production, or closed-loop process methodology, this sounding of the completion bell spurs further, more articulated development.

9. *Probe embedded qualities.* A fundamental truth is that people tend to develop that which their superiors value and measure. If we constantly stress current production, current sales, this quarter's results, and other short-term accomplishments, without giving attention or value to developing results, we will encourage short-term production and discount long-term potential. This being the case, anything we can do to promote and give credit for increased *potential* in addition to increased *production* will help develop human capital. This means we must probe for and show interest in embedded capital and qualities, and in developing, though not yet exploitable, capabilities. When we show interest in these assets, they tend to flourish. When we ignore or penalize them, they surely die.

Taking all these suggestions into account, then, the nurturing culture we need to pursue is dominated by investment in the future, attention to postponed needs as well as present ones, and a focus on management cultivation and regeneration at all levels within our organizations. The result is a much stronger, better-managed, and more change-responsive company. This is how and why human capital is developed.

The Nissan Example

The importance of human capital has not been lost in the new wave of foreign companies now establishing production facilities in the United States. When the giant Japanese automaker Nissan decided to build a truck assembly plant in America, one of its key siting considerations, besides local availability of workers and management, was the *adaptability* of the locals to the Nissan culture.

The social fabric, prevailing attitudes toward work and employers, and sense of community they found in middle Tennessee played a large part in their decision to select the small town of Smyrna for their plant. Not stopping there, they proceeded to integrate selected U.S. employees into their firm through countless exchange trips to Japan and orientation sessions in the United States.

Nissan realized that new manufacturing facilities and the most modern equipment must be coupled with a commensurate level of human capital in order to make their new venture viable. While they were designing and constructing their plant, they were nurturing and molding the soft property that would operate it. The end result is now considered by many a model of management-employee relations as well as a tremendously successful production facility. Toyota has recently selected a site in central Kentucky with the same objectives in mind.

Ways to Destroy Human Capital

As much as we need to know ways to develop human capital, we must confront those that destroy it as well. This is because oftentimes, though we do not consciously destroy our managerial potential, we do allow it to lapse, atrophy, and dissolve through lack of attention. Knowingly or not, most companies practice some form of repressive or benign destruction. Here's how they do it.

1. *Discount the human factor.* A most pervasive practice, this is the primary error of companies demonstrating an extractive culture. Subtle

ways in which this occurs include emphasis on hard properties, machinery, systems, procedures, and processes at the expense or to the neglect of management efforts and human contributions. A company culture so focused on *things* that it ignores *people* practices this form of destruction. Extractive leaders would rather people be fixed instead of adaptive; ascertainable rather than mysterious; and always giving, never demanding cultivation. They forget that no machine ever ran a division, managed a project, or made a sale. For these functions we need people.

2. *Encourage jurisdictional dispute.* Some managements view their most important role as some sort of jurisdictional referee, constantly tightening the borders surrounding specialization by promoting rivalry, individual advancement, and finite rewards. They seek to assign success or failure to someone or some group, even when either may have resulted from aggregate efforts or distributed contributions. This promotes narrow vision, champions the small picture, and cripples change consciousness.

3. *Maintain outdated impressions.* Many of us refuse to modify our impressions of others beyond that gained on initial exposure. We constantly view someone as he or she existed upon entering the company, no matter how much the person has developed since then. We "fix" capabilities and refuse to acknowledge or accommodate growth. Because we maintain these outdated impressions, we fail to give the individual more challenging assignments or broadened responsibilities.

Nurturing cultures not only foster growth but constantly search for its signs, giving advanced identities often and without begrudging anyone in the process. They celebrate advancement and announce it throughout the organization. In so doing they recognize that valuable people are by nature constantly seeking newer and higher identities, constantly seeking improvement and notice thereof. This is why many outstanding individuals leave a company and look for employment elsewhere: not because they want to establish a new identity but because they want the one they have already established to be recognized.

4. *Penalize development efforts.* When we keep managers, or any other employees, so tied down to a process, so busy producing for us now that they cannot afford the time to nurture their own development, we thereby destroy any chances that they will develop. Motivated managers are their own best handlers, seldom needing encouragement to grow, to generalize, to broaden. If we stifle this positive urge by restricting their training budgets, limiting their exposure to others, and keeping them on a subsistence diet of information, we will eventually lose them, through attrition or the atrophy of their drive. Even the most

ambitious employees eventually tire of beating their heads against a brick wall.

5. *Guard information.* That layered hierarchies often embody a culture that rewards secrecy is itself no secret. This is a problem well described by Green and Berry: "If the underpinning of hierarchy is knowledge about the enterprise, then each level has an 'investment' in the relative ignorance of those underneath" (1985, p. 32). Given a guaranteed market share, continuous demand for our products or services, and a comfortable profit margin, most companies could afford this underpinning. We know that businesschange allows us to rely on none of these variables. Information hoarding is a game for losers.

Adult workers and their managements aren't children who cannot be trusted with nonessential data. They appreciate exposure to management decision making even when they are not a part of it themselves. They appreciate knowing *why* something was done or is imminent in addition to merely *how* they are to implement it.

Tools, machines, and computers do not share this need; they need to be told only so much as absolutely and immediately required. People are different. Giving them what might be thought of as nonessential information demonstrates a nurturing attitude, promotes their generalized interest, and reaffirms their ability to handle more knowledge than that which a tool, machine, or computer needs.

6. *Punish deviates.* The more our managers' charters depend on rote procedure, specific instructions, and invariant processes, the more we foster a generation of compliers—human robots. Here we might heed the warning of Erich Fromm: "The danger of the past was that men became slaves. The danger of the future is that men may become robots" (1955, p. 312). There is little question that corporate goals and standards require some uniformity of control and consistency of management action, but beyond those absolutely essential, the rest are merely restrictions upon management prerogative.

By its very nature management represents the exercise of judgment, discretion, and situationally dependent reactions taken after due consideration of their consequences. If we take these away from a manager, the result is to have not a manager at all but a highly paid, well-regulated bureaucrat: a compliance drone. Compliance drones are not only lost as far as their own development is concerned, but they invariably foster compliance and penalize creativity among those under their command. Compliance drones breed more of their own kind. If we need a character to symbolize a human change target, the compliance drone is ideally suited for the role.

7. *Recognize only the visible.* Because it is difficult to see embedded qualities, or capital, as opposed to the attached variety, many companies fail to recognize it. They may admit its tangential value and delayed benefit, but they discount it by focusing only on that which may be measured. In some cases, they go so far as to try to quantify the qualitative nature of potential in a convoluted, artificial manner. This usually flattens potential to a single dimension—and we know that human potential, like change itself, loses all character when we flatten it or force it into quantitative clothing.

8. *Work 'em till they drop.* The height of extractive philosophy occurs among executives who view people as things to be used and discarded—ore to be mined. They view the world as an endless source of fresh material, new recruits, new employees who share the company's existing values and are eager to be exploited by the company. Should more or different capabilities be needed in light of changed conditions, such companies believe they can tap a figurative pipeline and fresh people, so suited, will spurt out of the faucet and willingly place themselves at the company's disposal.

It is not difficult to spot executives who hold this view. All we need to do is look at their personnel turnover and at the problems with and lack of development of people under their command. While these executives may succeed in the short term, particularly among these companies where the short term is the only term considered, they will surely fail once conditions change. They have forgotten that employees are not billiard balls—that people learn, investigate, and respond according to their internal drives as well as those offered by the company. A manager who eats the seed stock soon finds the feed bag empty.

9. *Allow a major change recalcitrant.* A "change recalcitrant" is someone who refuses to acknowledge, allow, or accommodate change. These people insist on fighting any proposed changes and ignoring those already made or inevitable. Change recalcitrants have been with industry since its beginning. In England during the nineteenth century, Luddites destroyed new textile equipment to prevent loss of jobs. And the word "sabotage" came into being as a result of a similar French movement in which workers tossed their wooden shoes (sabots) into machinery in order to destroy it and thus, they hoped, to keep its innovation away from the workplace. In *The Challenge of Hidden Profits*, Green and Berry describe "contemporary Luddites" who "include balky workers and union leaders, as well as white-collar managers who ignore the need to innovate" (1985, p. 185).

These terms are usually used to describe low-level production workers, but it is not uncommon to find change recalcitrants at middle and senior management positions, and this is where we have trouble. These managers cause massive damage in addition to simple aggravation of existing conditions. They stymie change consciousness among those around them or under their command, block the development of human capital, retard implementation of much-needed induced change, and generate a tremendous amount of jurisdictional dispute. In order to come to grips with change we must come to grips with those whose business fantasy is a world stopped and standing still for them.

Finding Managers Attuned to Change

Not everyone is a candidate for the challenging role of manager in change, nor is individual potential for capital development uniform and to be taken for granted. In a climate dominated by change we must take care to identify and select managers best suited to the climate, *attuned to change*. Here are their characteristics:

1. *Resourcefulness.* "Resourcefulness" is the ability to use whatever is at hand to further one's own position. Changing conditions often eliminate the obvious choice, the optimum method, and the most direct process. Managers who cling to specific processes or techniques, are comfortable only with the ideal, and are unable to extemporize do poorly in change. When we eliminate candidates for management, the first to go should be process zealots, who insist that their "one" way is the "only" way things can be done.

2. *Goal-orientation.* Resourceful managers are more often goal-oriented than process- or position-dependent. They embrace results rather than methods, choosing to *accomplish* rather than to *comply*. This is not to say they are always breaking the rules or deviating from them capriciously. To the contrary, they simply see rules as tools justified only by their effectiveness, and are not afraid to bend them or to develop new ones when the need arises. Goal-oriented managers recognize that the effect of change is to reduce the importance of any one process or tehnique and to increase the importance of success.

3. *Ability to synthesize.* Change immunity requires general perspectives and approaches and an ability to synthesize the disparate efforts and methods of specialty groups. Managers who excel in this capability help transcend the gaps and walls separating contributing parts from the higher whole. Not only is synthesis necessary, we seldom have time for it to occur under ideal, controlled conditions. It must be accomplished

rapidly and with as little internal friction as possible. To the extent that any one manager shows this ability, he or she will succeed in a world where it is sorely needed.

4. *Vision.* Change seldom sneaks up on our companies or attacks without warning. Astute managers constantly peer into the future, over the horizon of their immediate needs, in order to sense impending change and better prepare for it. This requires a special quality called *vision*, and the ability to change one's perspective from near to far and back again almost instantaneously. To develop and hone such a skill, managers must have broad interests and far-reaching concerns as opposed to special, narrow interests and shortsightedness.

5. *Nonlinearity.* We are often tempted to profile a candidate by specific skills, specific types of experience aligned with them, and a history of handling constant and improving responsibilities similar to those we will give the new manager. This expectation is a sort of *experience linearity* that tends to stifle generalization, focus on detailed optimization, and rule out candidates who have shown adaptation to be a strength. It might be better to select those who have succeeded in vastly differing settings, in changed conditions, and by so doing have demonstrated an ability to adapt, to transcend, and to quickly marshall their talents and focus them on different objectives. Nonlinearity of success demonstrates management adaptability and sustained confidence—attractive features for a manager facing change.

6. *Variable focus.* The knack of changing management focus or attention from the detailed to the summary, from the near term to the far term, and from the specific to the general increases a person's change immunity. In a sense, we can think of such a manager as posessing a variable-focus lens of attention, capable of zooming in and out frequently and clearly. Managers in change can readily shift from one area of concern to another, can relate to low-level production problems and to high-level strategic issues, and are often seen translating for others—helping them to make intuitive leaps from the big picture to the small component and vice versa.

7. *Reason.* Zealotry in any field of business, at any position, is sometimes confused with enthusiasm, loyalty, or dedication to our company and what it represents. The problem with this attribute is that it ties any such loyalty, enthusiasm, or dedication to a specific product, process, or technique. It clings to management variables which must often change, or be changed. This is the negative effect of zealotry: it creates fixity of process or purpose, which hampers adaptability to change.

Company zealots tend to force solutions on questions that haven't been asked, or to fit the work to the tools they so patriotically espouse and defend. They tend to ignore alternatives and to shut out changed circumstances. Managers attuned to change, however, know when to continue with what works; most important of all, they know when to *admit defeat*, let go, and move on. Their loyalty is to higher principles, such as company advancement, change immunity, long-term profitability, and viability, rather than to specific, temporary accoutrements in use today. Managers attuned to change are decidedly *nonzealous*. They are more accurately described as expedient, pragmatic, and reasonable. This doesn't mean they are not dedicated; they are just wise in selecting their objects of dedication.

Nurturing Adaptive Managers

If there is one prevailing misconception in most companies and among most managers, it is that the recruitment process ends once a candidate is hired or promoted. Nothing could be further from the truth. Recruitment of any individual is a continuous process, beginning with initial screening before employment and only ending when the individual has eventually left the firm. We must constantly identify, attract, and reward managers. They don't fix their impressions of our company upon employment and tear up their résumés because they won't be needing them again. On the contrary, every astute manager seeks the best for himself or herself at all times. People who don't do this aren't the type of manager most of us would prefer to have working for us. They are drones, not managers attuned to change.

To separate the winners from the losers requires a few basic steps in every company. Here are some.

1. *Continual recruitment.* We simply cannot fix a person's expectations, objectives, or value systems at any given time and presume to keep that person contented in the future by meeting them. Just as we must constantly vary our impression of each manager's capability (by continually revising the first impression), so should we revise our understanding of their expectations. This takes more than the traditional annual review. Expectations and objectives of managers attuned to change are modified much more frequently.

2. *Deferral to management judgment.* The content and substance of managers' daily work must excite and challenge them. For generalists, and those with expedient, product-oriented vision, we need to provide general guidelines and to give wide latitude to their individual management discretion. Rote procedures and a compliance mentality are anath-

ema to these people. They prefer to use their own creativity, imagination, and resourcefulness (those attributes we so highly value during the recruitment process) rather than to comply with existing procedures without question.

Resourcefulness, creativity, and imagination must be continually exercised, or they will soon atrophy. We cannot allow this to happen, for we will need these qualities in the future, when things are going to change.

3. *Frequent appraisals.* Progressive managers do not like to perform for extended periods of time without any process feedback, readouts, or intermediate accomplishment. They constantly scan their environments for indications of how well they are doing, because they know that process- or position-dependent confidence, though comforting, is unresponsive to change. Process zealots need little encouragement or orientation, for they "know" they are doing well as long as they perform the process that is "best." They see no reason to take intermediate readouts or to identify intermediate accomplishments.

Managers attuned to change, then, need lighter leashes (looser procedures, etc.) and *shorter* ones. This is not because we don't trust them to proceed for longer durations, but because *they* want to know how well they are doing at intermediate points along their journey. To give them a long, unresponsive leash is tantamount to programming their activity.

4. *Recognizing group accomplishments.* Parcelled-out nurture, that given only to selected individuals, is no different from favoritism. We must encourage and allow our managers to nurture those around and below them. We do this by insisting on group leverage rather than individual success, and by measuring not merely what a manager has done, but what that manager has allowed others to do.

5. *Recognizing barriers.* Whenever a significant accomplishment takes place within the limitations and risks generated by change, we need not only to acknowledge the accomplishment but to enunciate the barriers surmounted, the difficulties transcended, and the setbacks overcome on the road to the accomplishment. Seldom is significant progress made without difficulty. We should let our managers know that we fully recognize the difficulties they have faced, and we should reward accomplishment by enunciating barriers overcome.

6. *Providing ancillary information.* Successful managers hone their adaptive skills and broaden their peripheral vision by ingesting a great deal of information, particularly information that goes beyond maintenance of their knowledge at subsistence levels. They crave ancillary knowledge, different perspectives, and general exposure. To fill this

need, we must provide them with much more than they require for their immediate functions. In particular, they expect to be told *why* something is done, in addition to *what* and *how*.

7. *Rewarding transcendence.* To nurture generalists, we must recognize and reward, rather than punish, attempts at building bridges, transcending specialty barriers, and creating environments in which many, not a few, may succeed. Managers successful in change seldom succeed alone or with small groups closely aligned with them. Instead they succeed jointly, with the participation of many others, often including very different organizations holding very different value systems. Pragmatic, expedient managers do not ignore different approaches that may contribute to success.

8. *Recognizing multiple accomplishments.* Managers attuned to change show a preference for multiple accomplishments as opposed to singular optimization. We should recall that, beyond a certain point, optimization of any singular product, process, or technique exacts penalties and costs in change immunity. We need managers who can help us improve on many fronts, advance many capabilities, and develop many different opportunities, rather than managers only able to perfect a single function. Regardless of the incremental value such perfection may bring, it could ultimately represent the mere polishing of a change target. Again, most of us would rather have a manager with a 90 percent success rate in five areas than with a 99 percent success rate in only one. This capability is what separates "managers" from narrow-scope "individual contributors."

Developing Contrasts

Being business pragmatists, most of us choose the object and amount of any investment by considering the character of the investment opportunity. We view human capital as offering more or less, depending on our perspective, of an investment potential than other choices, including hard and soft properties. But change modifies our views, creating newer, more adaptive attitudes. These new views often demonstrate an increased value in human capital and an increased willingness to nurture it. Old views, those insensitive to the effects of change, cling to the notion that nonhuman capital is the best investment. Here are some additional contrasts between the old and the new investment attitudes:

Old Views	New Views
Better tools make better workers.	Better workers make better tools.
People are a liability.	People are an asset.
Humans bring uncertainty.	Humans bring adaptability.
Objects have specific utility.	People have general capability.
Things can be measured and priced.	People bring immeasurable, priceless value.
Equipment requires maintenance.	People require nurturing.
Things wear out when used.	People atrophy when ignored.
Machines bring value because they don't change.	Humans bring value because they can change.
We depend on the certainty of nonhuman resources.	We are certain that humans can be resourceful.

The Prices and Risks of Human Investment

Despite the tremendous benefit human capital brings, it is not without price, nor can we invest in people without assuming general and specific risks. The continuing challenge such investment requires of every company represents the most common and extensive costs we may face. That people are best seen as "rented" rather than "bought" (despite some misconceptions to the contrary) forces us to give them constant attention and nurture. We must never presume to take ownership for granted, but must recruit our best managers continually, not just as a prerequisite to their employment. They represent not only a first cost but one we must continually pay.

Other prices are the difficulties of tying investment to effect and of directly correlating increments of investment and effect. It is therefore almost impossible to justify additional funds for development without *trusting* that they will be well spent. Most managements consider trust a heavy price to pay; we are more comfortable with clearly quantifiable prices.

The inability to measure or account for investment in human capital has long been its greatest obstacle. Thoreau put his pen to it over a century ago, when he wrote "But man's capacities have never been measured; nor are we to judge of what he can do by any precedents, so little has been tried" (1964, p. 11). In more recent times, noted economist John Kenneth Galbraith, in his famous work *The Affluent Society*, addressed the problem in his own fashion (1969, p. 262):

> Since investment in individuals, unlike investment in a blast furnace, provides a product that can be neither seen nor valued, it is inferior. And here

the conventional wisdom unleashes its epithet of last resort. Since these achievements are not easily measured, as a goal, they are "fuzzy."

An admitted problem with human investment is that it is placed in a mobile object—one with two legs and capable of leaving at any time. The truth is, however, that the less we invest in people, the more likely they are to leave, and conversely, carefully nurtured, they are more likely to stay. Rather than expose us to loss (because those in whom we invest can take that investment with them), a failure to invest almost assures loss.

For those managements holding a very tight grip on every aspect of company operations, investing in the judgment of others is a difficult practice to accept. Limited autonomy, shorter and lighter leashes, and less reliance on enforcement of restrictions are also prices we must pay in order to develop responsible managers equipped to deal with change. To the extent that decentralized operations and greater autonomy at lower levels conflict with any company's existing culture, that company will find it difficult to meet the needs of managers attuned to change.

Without question, investment in human capital relies on confrontation with people, both the kind of people who help us in changing conditions and those who frustrate our attempts at becoming immune to change. To improve our chances of dealing successfully with change, we must rid our staffs of change recalcitrants. This is more difficult than ridding ourselves of an unwanted or outmoded machine. Machines don't look us in the eye. To profit through people, we must not only cherish the seeds but remove the weeds.

7

Closing the Gaps in Intimacy

Demanding management proximity

*The role of manager is also one of
alienation. It is true, he manages the whole
and not a part, but he too is alienated from
his product as something concrete and useful.*
ERICH FROMM

To profit through change you must become *proximate*. This is true because the closer one is to that which is changing, the easier it is to recognize and exploit change. It is this condition of closeness, of intimacy with whatever aspect of business we are hoping to perform, understand, or control, that we call "management proximity." As management proximity increases, the factors that distort our observation, interject disturbing noise, and confuse our understanding of causes and effects are weakened or eliminated. As we draw away from the objects of our attention, in the dimensions of space and time, the filtering and blurring caused by these factors increases. Lack of proximity is the condition of being distant, removed, and apart from. Most alienation between a manager and the work is caused not by lack of understanding or effort but by lack of proximity.

A number of steps are now being taken by several companies not only to enhance management proximity but to require it. Some of these steps are cultural and others are structural. Regardless of the particular manifestation, proximity is fast becoming inseparable from the concept of management itself. Some of the following signposts spring from this conclusion.

Signposts of Change

- **Decentralized, flatter company organizations.** Pyramids of power belong with division of labor, fixity of process, and linear functions. In other words, they belong in the past. Flatter organizations push management down to the work. They represent the structure of proximity.

- **Emphasis on management participation rather than regulation.** Managers can no longer afford to be only witnesses or regulators. They must join in the effort. Companies in change can't afford vestigial executives. As Francis Bacon said over 300 years ago, "Men ought to know that in the theatre of human life it is only for Gods and angels to be spectators" (quoted by Durant, 1953, p. 114). Most companies have neither.

- **Physical relocation of managers to the workplace.** Spatial separation invites loss of perspective and control. To manage in change we must go to the workplace.

- **Fewer insulating executive perks (dining rooms, suites, assistants, furniture, first-class travel, etc.).** Time, distance, and attitude are the key factors of proximity. Problems with time and distance can be overcome by purchasing an airline ticket or an on-line information system. Attitude problems are much more difficult to resolve.

- **More frequent traveling for managers.** Decentralization, outsourcing, worldwide facilities and markets, and subcontracted work are forcing many of us to take an airplane to work each day.

- **Less patience with management information systems.** If a system or gadget doesn't add proximity, we are likely to toss it aside or look around it rather than through it. The business world is full of executives with 150-pound electronic paperweights on their desks.

- **More direct process observation.** More time is being spent watching what we're in charge of rather than reading reports about it. Being proximate means getting on top of our work, not peering at its shadows.

- **Greater delegation of responsibility and authority.** To bring the manager and the "managed" together, we are passing the management function down the side of the organizational pyramid. If the work or the people can't be moved, the decision surely can.

- **More egalitarian work forces and working conditions**.   Physical contact and real-time participation are the greatest levelers of status and class. Muddy wing tips look very similar to muddy work boots.

Proximity and the Management Effect

Even under the most ideal, static conditions, our perceptions are weakened or exaggerated by external and internal forces and biases, making it difficult to ascertain exactly what is happening and why it is happening. This distortion is intensified by limitations in our viewing and measuring apparatus, by our finite management focus, and by our inability to deal with more than just a handful of concepts or features at any given time. Not only is our perception muted, but our management actions are transformed, misdirected, and misapplied due to a lack of management proximity. Our *management effect* is lost or altered to the point where it bears no resemblance to our original intentions, which themselves may have been inappropriate because of distortions in our perception and understanding.

The problems of obscured perception and garbled effect become even greater when we and the objects of our management effort move to dynamic conditions. The propensity of change to dilate, contract, float, and defy cause-and-effect analysis contribute, as do the fluidity of our environment and the unsynchronized motion of the manager and the "managed"—motion that is commonly nonuniform, nonlinear, and unpredictable.

It is particularly essential, in times of change, to draw closer in time and space to that which we manage—to *gain proximity*. Increased proximity helps us detect change with minimum distortion and take effective action with minimum interference. Together, the abilities to *understand* and to *affect* represent the essence of the management function. Proximity clarifies perception and guides effect; it's that simple.

At the Races

A person wishing to control the outcome of a horse race is least proximate if he reviews the racing news, say, 2 weeks after the event and in an office hundreds of miles from the track. To increase proximity this person could (1) read the news of the race sooner, (2) listen to the race broadcast over the radio, (3) watch the race live on television, (4) watch the actual race from the grandstand, (5) move to the rail and shout commands and encouragement to the jockey, and finally, (6) ride the horse. Each of these steps brings the "racing manager" closer in time or distance and reduces the effect of lags, float, and distortion, progressively changing the person from a distant observer to an actual participant.

While a business manager is "in the saddle," proximity is also at its peak. The manager senses changes in the horse, the pace, the track, and the competition, and gets immediate, undiluted feedback on the effect of his or her own actions: posture, grip on the reins, use of the whip. Understanding and control are direct and are intimately entwined, the process loop is strong and closed, the manager is fully aware and totally in charge—"in control" in the fullest meaning of the phrase.

In an ideal environment, we would each be riding our own horse rather than reading about the race outcome or even exhorting the surrogate jockey from the stands. Except for the lowest level of performers, this is impossible; for as one progresses from production up through higher levels of management, proximity becomes more and more tested and difficult to achieve. Most managers dream with fondness of such simple objectives and conditions—riding one horse in one race with one goal: to finish first.

In reality we each must see that several horses, in many contests at many times and locations, are winning. And our management charter and reach cover not simply the race itself, but the purchase of horses, their care and training, the selection of jockeys and races, the operation of support facilities, and (to add insult to injury) the insurance and tax ramifications of each decision. Perhaps this is why so many executives enjoy simple pastimes and basic hobbies while off duty. They are attracted to sports, sailing, woodworking, gardening, and the like—not because these activities resemble their work, but because they don't. In dealing with the racket, the boat, the saw, or the shovel, the executive finds pure, unadulterated proximity to the object: that which is so elusive at the office or the plant.

Absentee Landlords

If you ever want to witness the negative results of proximity loss, simply find a business establishment where the owner is never around, lives elsewhere, or is otherwise removed. People perform their functions (or don't), equipment is used, and processes are conducted, but there is no equity-enhanced interest to make sure the result is obtained. The land-lord is absent and the place quickly goes to hell.

We all know the best restaurants are those where the owner is in the kitchen or in the dining room with the patrons, there to spot those nonfunctionally specific problems that require correction.

Some franchise agreements even specify a minimum amount of "store time" to be spent by the franchisee. McDonald's used to require a min-imum of 40 hours a week in the store by each owner. This not only assured management proximity for each store, but since few owners could spend more than 60 to 80 hours a week working, it kept them from buying more stores than they could *physically manage*. Not a bad way to guarantee proximity, which, after all, is little more than assuring our reach doesn't exceed our grasp.

But is proximity something that can be gained simply by putting in so many hours in the store, on the shop floor, or in the field? Or are other elements involved? Perhaps it's time we explored this condition more carefully.

Understanding the Nature of Proximity

If we think of the management function as a closed loop which, when employed by capable individuals, brings about continuous enhancement, correction, and application of the management effect, then the two es-sential segments of that loop are *perception* and *control*. Perception is the ability to discern what exists, or is about to exist, in a clear, undistorted manner. Control is the exercise of induced change consistent with what we perceive and with our intentions. No matter what business we are in or what our personal management charter, our management function is more effective when these two segments are short and direct—when the object is closer to the observer and manipulator: the manager. Prox-imity clarifies perception and helps target control.

Management proximity, then, helps us see and feel, helps us *sense* what is happening without undue reliance on artificial or contrived *te-lemetry*. Telemetry systems, whether they are manual reports or on-line automated information loops, are simply props that aid us in seeing or sensing. At best, they are substitutes when direct observation is difficult or impossible to attain. Merely management aids, no such system is needed unless it increases perception, and none is constructed without compromise or without tradeoffs between cost and benefit. Like man-agement models, telemetry systems are artificial replacements for what is preferred: unadulterated direct observation. To the extent that they transmit pure, undistorted information on our business operations, they are valuable. When they contain built-in filters, or transducers, and show a propensity to contract, dilate, or distort change, they become liabilities.

The products of telemetry are all around every business office. They include computer printouts, sales receipts, survey results, time sheets, audit findings, performance reports, and verbal briefings. If the manager were actually in the saddle of the enterprise, none of these would be necessary. But as mentioned before, this would make us performers rather than managers, jockeys rather than owners of a racing syndicate. There is no question in the minds of jockeys about their position in the conversion process or the objectives and conditions thereof. They enjoy complete proximity, they do not suffer from alienation. Managers do suffer, however, and our suffering increases as we become more and more removed from the horse, the whip, and the track. We must rely on telemetry.

A condition that counters alienation and is associated with increased proximity is achieved when individual managers see themselves as part of the work, as essential to the outcome. Those who feel that they are mere "attachments" to an otherwise self-sustaining enterprise have lost all proximity and all justification for the title of "manager," particularly in times of change. Management is an essential element of every process, and not an exalted appendage thereto.

In order to fulfill the role of management, then, we must be quickly aware of and responsive to events, as they change. We must not become the victims of faulty telemetry. We need to anticipate changes rather than simply react to them once they have occurred. And we must always recognize the proper place and temporary nature of the tools we use to increase proximity, understanding their fallibility and weaknesses.

The term "management scaffolding" describes the tools we use in both observing and controlling our companys' conversion processes. All such management scaffolding, like its physical counterparts, exists only to allow us to see and reach that which is difficult to access without it. Indeed, like physical scaffolding, management scaffolding is hastily erected to allow people to gain proximity to their work. It brings managers closer to our work and the work closer to us. Any reports, surveys, briefings, or automated systems that do not serve this function are mere clutter.

We must constantly be aware of the limitations of scaffolding and must never rely completely on the information thus obtained. From time to time it pays to look beyond our viewing apparatus; to peer over the microscope or to the side of the telescope; and to determine whether the reports we are getting are correct, accurate, and without filter or distortion. Or we may occasionally need to use alternate information-gathering tools and compare the results with those previously attained.

Such approaches help us separate what is real from distortions caused simply by our methods of viewing. It helps us test our telemetry and judge our scaffolding, none of which should be taken for granted.

As we appraise each business tool, management information system, or model, we should consider its ability to give not only an accurate view but one that is well-rounded, fully developed, and complete. If it is doing these things for us, it is an excellent system, a good substitute for physical proximity. If not, it is our enemy in the costume of a tool. As surely as some tools enhance or subsitute for proximity, others impede it. Astute managements look at any proposed or existing apparatus with a good deal of healthy skepticism. They understand the weakness of telemetry and quickly determine which elements create distance rather than reduce it.

Because proximity is essential to management and because it becomes much more difficult to attain under changing conditions, we must attack whatever works against it. Some threats to proximity are fairly obvious, but others are deceptive and subtle, often buried under layers of perceived benefit or misunderstanding.

Organizational Strata

Translation of data from one person or system to another carries with it an inherent filtering and distortion effect. Third-hand information is usually more *interpreted*, more biased, and more removed from reality than direct, first-hand versions. The "rolling up" of information from one management level to higher ones and the subsequent "cascading down" of directions through the same layers tend to cause blur and distortion, not to mention dilation, contraction, and simple time float. Highly tiered, pyramidal organizations requiring this upward and downward translation invite loss of proximity. They are often characterized by "a trickle-down style of management where orders issued from above slowly pass down, losing direction and authority all along the way. In bureaucratese it's known as 'line loss'" (Green & Berry, 1985, p. 20).

Centralized decision making also causes data to be handed off from one level to another, as they pass from the extremities of the company (where the conversion processes are actually performed) in toward the center of decision making and back out to the operating units. Steep organizational pyramids and highly centralized authority work against proximity. Distortion and loss of understanding and effect take place on both paths of the management loop, as information travels up and down or into and out of the organization. Each organizational layer encountered along this journey tends to delay, misinterpret, filter, and sometimes compress what is known or what is to be done. The net line loss can be phenomenal.

Two factors seem to be at work here, one supporting or prolonging the viability of pyramidal organizations and the other destroying it. A problem with highly centralized structures has been the inability to close the information loop, to summarize planning and performance data upward through successive layers and to send management policies and commands downward. At some critical mass the flow has been interrupted or the garbling and time lags have become intolerable. Thus, highly structured organizations have tended to limit themselves by the flow of data through them. Not so anymore. The advent of automated reporting systems and on-line process manipulation seems to have removed this informational obstacle, allowing even more structured organizations to persist.

On the other hand, there is everywhere, in business and society as a whole, a strong tendency toward decentralization. According to Naisbitt, "Centralized structures are crumbling all across America. . . . The decentralization of America has transformed politics, business, our very culture" (1982, p. 97). One can only hope that decentralization will prevail—that the computer will assist in our quest for proximity and join the chorus of forces, most of them allied with the phenomenon of change, calling for the proximity that decentralized businesses afford.

Telemetry Systems

Undue or sole reliance on substitutes for first-hand observation, for intimacy, for proximity, carries many dangers. This is not to cast doubt on the value of sophisticated, computer-based information systems. Let's distinguish between two typical functions of these systems before relating each to the subject of proximity.

Certain businesses must handle a great deal of information as part of their conversion processes. This we call "transaction-related information," and transaction systems process it. Banks using computers to facilitate deposit recording, account maintenance, customer inquiries, and transfer activity typically use advanced automated systems. These systems have little or nothing to do with management information, however; they simply replace clerical functions that would otherwise perform the work. Airlines use similar automated computer systems to book reservations, assign routes, position aircraft, and load cargo in the most efficient manner. These systems are part of the work of an airline, making the conversion process possible.

Management information systems, on the other hand, exist only to tell managers what is happening with processes, how results compare with standards or plans, and how efficient the processes are and how well or poorly they are being performed. A management information system is an *appendage*. It is not essential to the daily work process; it exists to substitute for proximity so that the process can be understood and manipulated by management. These systems must be judged on whether they contribute to or detract from the management effect. Anyone who needs to decide on the merits of a computer-based information system, therefore, must be able to distinguish between the transaction elements and the management information capabilities. The efficiency, accuracy, and dependability inherent in transaction processing should not be confused with the higher levels of proximity they may or may not provide.

The Personal Computer: Tool or Obstacle?

Here lies the greatest danger and the brightest promise of the personal computer (PC) in business. The danger is that it will place yet another obstacle in the path of proximity—a technological marvel adding more distance or yet another filter between the manager and what needs to be managed. Should we become infatuated with the tool (and thereby distracted from its purpose), limited in outlook by its capabilities (looking only at that which it shows), or misled into confusing reality with its mimicry on a video display unit, proximity will take a nosedive.

The promise, however, is bright because the PC has the ability to bring performance information directly to the manager (avoiding the data processing department, or the unofficial "information guards" found in most large organizations). It also does an excellent job of compressing or collapsing the change float that threatens the viability of all management information. To the extent that the PC can show change directly, untainted by organizational or time constraints, it may prove to be the foundation of a new age of proximity.

Status, Perks, and Distance

Not only our tools but our own actions and attitudes filter and distort our vision. If we remain in the office, we do not see what is going on in the field or on the shop floor. It we are specialists in time management, we may not perceive inefficiencies encountered by improper material selection. If we speak only with vice presidents and staff advisers, we shut out any valuable information originating at lower levels of the organization. This is because, apart from the use of any systems or observation tools, every manager is an observer at heart. As such, our lens is often of fixed focus, our viewing position is often immobile, and our ability to detect patterns is often limited to those we are comfortable with or readily recognize because of our education or experience.

What this means is that the management effect of any one manager is limited, and this limitation can only be overcome by using more than one manager to view any given object. It takes more than one viewing position for the human eye to detect distance (this is why we have two eyes, for depth perception), and it often takes more than one manager's impression to detect change.

Homogenizing Information

Because impressions, however gained, are subjectively processed, we have difficulty communicating them to others without converting them to some sort of quantifiable basis—without unitizing them to some extent. We should recognize that this limits the *variability of information* to one or two dimensions. Sending quantitative data up and down the company chain of command is like homogenizing food; only the amount varies, and no distinctions are made between different appearances, flavors, textures or nutritive values. Processed and transcribed information loses character, quality, and personality. It limits our perception to one sense and makes that which is perceived bland, flat, and sterile.

Learning in Many Dimensions

Let's return to our earlier example: the sale of salt. Suppose you are the product manager and sense that a newer, more attractive package may boost sales. You could redesign the container, place the new boxes on supermarket shelves, and tabulate any increase or decrease in sales (changes you could attribute to the new design) as compared to the old package. This information, though highly accurate and beyond dispute, would give you some understanding of the effectiveness of the new design; but it would be a very limited, one-dimensional understanding, based solely on quantitative data.

Suppose, instead, that you unobtrusively positioned an observer (perhaps the package designer) in various test supermarkets. This observer would be able to watch customers as they passed the display, considered the purchase, and either accepted or rejected the new design. In so doing, the observer could ascertain a great deal more than simply how much more or less was bought. Increased proximity would tell what types of customers bought the product, how they were dressed, and what lifestyle predominated; as well as whether the customers were predominantly men or women, old or young, affluent or not, hurried or deliberate; and whether they bought on impulse or carefully read the label. In addition, your observer would be able to find out whether your customers examined neighboring competitors or went for your product at once, and what other types of products they were buying during the same shopping trip. Many more qualitative impressions would be thus gained, and any one of these might bring to the surface the *affective essence* of the change—i.e., which elements of the package design seemed to work and which were merely noise.

Your observer could also determine the nature of those customers who did not examine or accept the new package, the effects of shelf positioning on purchases, and, if the observation period was long enough, the nature of repeat buyers. None of this valuable information would find its way into sales reports; it would be lost without increased proximity.

The point of this example is not to imply that quantitative data are useless, for they do in fact tell us the "bottom line" of a change: how much more or less is sold after it occurs. But proximity tells us *why, how,* and *when* sales are made, as well as *to whom, in what fashion,* and *in correlation with what else.* It also tells us about the sales that were not made and helps us ascertain why not. It allows us to feel all the distinct effects of the change deeply, rather than to simply weigh one aspect.

Management Hubris

For whatever reason, certain managers feel that to put distance between themselves and what they purport to manage somehow enhances their status. They view the trappings of proximity (muddy boots, rolled-up sleeves, intimate knowledge of the job workings) as representing lower-level interests and concerns.

The higher up the organization such managers rise, the more aloof they appear from the "skunk works" that generate their salary and afford them their attitudes. They wish to remain above "all that" and often view loss of proximity as an executive perk. These managers may also see proximity as *vulnerability* and thus may tend to avoid associating too closely with processes, concepts, or projects that may fail or fall out of favor. What they do not understand is that far from being a benefit of advancing status, loss of proximity is a penalty thereof. It only makes them expendable. The executives with the least proximity are those least essential. They are not integral to the company effort, but merely appurtenances. Loss of proximity is the most dangerous of perks.

The need for business leaders to become proximate, to shake off the tendency toward isolation that their positions naturally engender, is addressed by Peters and Waterman quite well. In describing successful leaders, they write, "These leaders believe, like an evangelist, in constantly preaching the 'truth,' not from their office but away from it—in the field. They travel more, and they spend more time, particularly with juniors, down the line" (1982, p. 288).

Seeking One's Own Level

Some managers have difficulty communicating with or relating to managers or performers at levels not identical with their own. These people are often seen in close proximity with other managers of the same status, and they are loath to mingle with others of different status.

The ability to change focus and attention from one organizational setting or concern to another is critical for change immunity, and essential to the condition of proximity. We must be able to zoom in and out, approach and recede, in order to maintain appropriate focus and effect. Those unable to transcend their own positions make poor managers in general, and even poorer managers in change. They belong in the world of bloated bureaucracy, where "their silly status symbols, like executive lunchrooms, parking spaces, elevators and washrooms, set up needless barriers between people" (Green & Berry, 1985, p. 28).

Transducers

"Transducers" are devices which convert one form of energy or information to another. We use transducers in almost every business communication. When a clerk records time spent by workers at a construction site, a perception of actual hours worked by each person is transformed into a written approximation and recorded on a time sheet. A cash register transforms actual purchases into a simple list of prices charged, cash tendered, and change refunded. An internal audit report translates an auditor's perceptions and observations into specific findings and recommendations demanding management attention. Regional sales reports translate thousands of transactions into specific categories, each quantified according to volume and revenue.

At each step employing a transduction there is natural slip, error, and lag in the complete transfer of information from input to output, from receiving to discharging elements. Management telemetry systems composed of a number of "information legs" joined together by transducers are susceptible to tremendous distortion, amplification, or dampening. Transducers are the junctions or joints in management scaffolding, and most reconfigure information as it passes through them.

This phenomenon is seen on both paths of the management loop—on both the incoming and the outgoing routes—for it affects our perception of events and our direction of induced change based on them. This is why the most simple, direct, and basic information telemetry is the most reliabile and most proximate. Whenever multiple transformations, summarizations, allocations, or representations are required, static and dynamic data are changed.

Hoarded Responsibility

Proximity often involves bringing an object closer to the manager, so that perception is enhanced and management intervention can occur without dampening, amplification, or misdirection. We can also increase proximity by bringing the *management decision* closer to the object. That is, rather than erecting cumbersome and float-filled scaffolding to transmit information to and from a distant manager, or paying the premiums of limited scope, view, and effect caused by bringing the manager closer to a given object, we can bring the *decision apparatus* closer by vesting it in a closer manager—a subordinate who, if not actually riding the horse, is close enough to communicate with the jockey directly. All this means is that, as responsibility to detect and determine what is going on is handed down to lower and lower levels within the organization, management proximity is increased. We need not always relocate or transpose the object or the viewer; sometimes we can instead transfer the *need to view* to a closer position.

This in mind, it is easy to see why retention of authority at higher levels runs counter to the demands of management proximity and creates even higher reliance on expensive, often untrustworthy telemetry. It is simply more difficult to manage the horse if the reins are being pulled from the executive suite and the whip is being wielded through wide gaps in distance and time. A better way to overcome the proximity dilemma is to give the reins and the whip to the jockey. Distributed responsibility, with commensurate authority, is a suitable way to satisfy the need for proximity. Companies which hoard authority at high levels, clenching it tightly to a few chests, lose in the game of proximity—especially when the game is played according to the rules of change.

Ways to Enhance Proximity

There is little doubt that proximity is a key issue to those managers attuned to change. They fully recognize the strength of direct and reliable information paths and the benefits of closeness to that which they manage. What many fail to see, however, are discrete, specific steps which any company can take to increase proximity without putting a heavy toll on their budgets or running counter to their cultures. The first step, of course, is to recognize the criticality of the issue and to appreciate why change makes proximity even more essential. Once this understanding is achieved, we can move on to those attitudes and techniques which foster this condition and away from those which impede it.

Closing Physical and Time Gaps

Nothing separates more than distance and time. We can easily increase proximity by bringing the manager (or the management function, such as the decision-making authority) closer to the business element being managed. This often involves relocating physically, making frequent trips to the field, abandoning the security of the home office or the executive suite, and being unafraid of a little mud on one's wing tips.

Time separates us from our work as well, making us alienated as surely as does tremendous spatial difference. To the extent that reports can be issued more frequently, telephones can be used instead of letters, measurements can be made more often, and briefings held soon after their subjects transpire, we can attempt to transcend the barriers of time.

An inherent fault of any management function is that it must be conducted in a series of steps rather than continually. We must perceive, change; perceive, change; perceive, change—and we are forced to act in a segmented series of steps, rather than continually perceiving and changing concurrently. The management function is articulated this way, never fluid or continuous. Life, on the other hand, is an ever-flowing continuum. The more closely the function can mimic the reality it attempts to control, the better. This often requires smaller, more frequent observations and manipulations, to bring what we see and what we know closer in time to what we are managing, reducing the ability of change to contrast, dilate, and float.

Peripheral Vision

"Peripheral vision" is the ability to see that which we are not peering at directly. It represents sensing that takes place on the fringes of our field of view, on the borders of our particular concern. It doesn't replace direct observation, but it does supplement and enhance what we actually see.

The primary value of peripheral vision is that it allows us to take in more than we think we need to know at any given time. This is especially helpful when we consider that change often occurs beyond or outside our field of vision, on the borders. We see motion by seeing the background change in relation to an object, and this observation can occur only on the border of the object.

Here again, what is nonessential or even distractive to "optimum" activity is essential for "adaptive" activity. Peripheral vision doesn't lend a thing to our ability to see what we are looking at, but it does a great deal to help us perceive conditions and changes on which we have not focused. It is best thought of as another dimension of proximity, for the closer we get to our object, the narrower our field of vision tends to be. Peripheral vision helps counteract this negative effect of proximity, by keeping our scope broad and our sensitivity general.

Traceability

Summarized information received at intermediate or higher levels of management often defies *traceability*. That is, we cannot trace effects which show up on our reports back to their original sources. The transduction, allocation, and truncation of quality that takes place in the reporting pipeline often flattens character and smudges distinctive features. We know something is wrong but cannot find out, at least via our telemetry, why it is wrong or from whence it came.

Any information systems which maintain the personality, the integrity, of information as it travels up and down the organizational pyramid are therefore to be cherished. Management reports which destroy the integrity of the information are only historical records of what has transpired rather than active parts of the management function. The manager with only historical information becomes an archivist rather than an effective intervenor.

Adjustable Models

Models with a fixed focus, fixed field, and fixed methodology are limited under dynamic conditions. The problem is that, because they are fixed, they do not show that change is occurring and that the model must therefore be jettisoned or reconfigured. Fixed models show fixity. What's needed in their place is adjustable models; models for which we can select a degree of coarseness or fineness; models which we can quickly point in different directions, focus on different levels of work, and adjust as changes dictate.

Any company or organizational unit that insists on one plan, one procedure, one report structure, one budgeting methodology, or the like has thereby fixed and shackled its management apparatus to one given time, set of conditions, and management need. Proximity is a relative condition, and as our object moves and shifts we must respond accordingly. This requires the adjustable analog, the general perspective, and the vigilant attitude. All foster an ability to detect just how close or distant we should be and allow us to quickly change proximity if it exacts too high a price or provides too little a reward.

Releasing Authority

Shifting management responsibility and authority downward, outward, or wherever it needs to go in order to be closer to the business need is a sensible response to the proximity problem. Some consider this done when lower-level managers become the "eyes and ears" of their superiors (*perception instruments*, the first part of management scaffolding), or even the "arms" of their superiors (*intervention instruments*, the other side of management scaffolding). But a lower-level manager in such a case simply becomes a human transducer, a soft link in the management telemetry stretching from the same object to the same manager and back again. In order to truly bring the decision making down (or out) to the most proximate level, upper-level managers must use subordinates not merely as their eyes, ears, and arms, but as their brains as well. The management function is then carried out *by* the lower-level managers rather than simply *through* them.

Developing Contrasts

It is impossible to quantify management proximity, to rank each manager on a scale from most to least proximate. We can, however, judge proximity in a subjective way, based on the signals given off by our managers and their activities. When you look for evidence of proximity or lack thereof in your specific business environment, the following contrasts may become evident.

Symptoms of Proximity Loss	*Signs of Proximity Gain*
Voluminous reports	Meaningful, reader-friendly reports
Disregard for details	Interest in revealing details
Stacked, layered managements	Linear, lean managements
Crowded offices, empty shops	Empty offices, crowded shops
A plethora of memoranda	Many hallway discussions
A strong and long chain of command	A few simple links
Executives meeting together	Executives listening to workers
Massive management information systems	Direct exposure and observation

The Prices and Risks of Demanding Management Proximity

Increased management proximity, as essential and change-sensitive as it may be, is difficult to achieve and costly to pursue. It commonly involves tradeoffs and penalties that may, at times, outweigh any incremental value it brings. Whether this occurs or not, it always requires effort and sacrifice and usually presents clear dangers to those not aware of its risks.

The most obvious of these is the possibility that managers, in an attempt to gain proximity, may become much too intimate with the details of the work, overly attached to the conversion process or technique used, and therefore unable to manage objectively. This is a common error of junior management and those still locked in a specialist frame of reference. Unless they are able to use a figurative "zoom lens," able to shift attention into and out of the details, they may get lost among the leaves and be unable to manage the forest.

The more proximate we become, the closer we get to real people, real pressures, and the possibility of real mistakes. Remaining at the distant end of a transducer-laden telemetry chain—reading summarized, homogenized reports couched in sanitary, quantifiable terms, and issuing orders into the end of the information pipeline—is much easier and more straightforward than dealing with real people face to face.

It is safer to manipulate scaffolding than to work with people and the events that surround their working lives. If you are unable to work with real people and real events, you should *invest* in businesses rather than purport to *manage* them. You may then get no closer to the business than the stock quotations, and may never have to pay the price of proximity: looking into the eyes of the people who create the dividends.

There are some managers who like cumbersome, deficient telemetry and control scaffolding for purposes not altogether altruistic. Poor information, nonresponsive systems, and excessively neutral information are all common scapegoats for management inaction or ignorance. How many times have we heard the phrase "If I had only been told of this earlier" as an attempt to evade culpability. Managers who profit in change take it upon themselves to find out what is really going on, by whatever means necessary and often by more than one means. This usually requires movement, action, and risk assumption. Proximity demands no less.

True proximity is egalitarian, stripping away unnecessary distinctions as we *all* chase better and more up-to-date information and effects. Managers who use lack of proximity as a status symbol belong in the world of fixed constants, where nothing changes and therefore no one needs to get too near the operation except those performing it. The world of fixed constants is the past, and those who were well suited to it are now extinct.

Transducers often interfere with rather than assist communication, and many transducers are of the human variety—real people. They often go by such names as "assistants," "staff specialists," "deputies," "analysts," and "administrators."

Many executives place one or more transducers between themselves and the outside world. Increasing proximity means that these transducers often become superfluous. Rather than continuing to depend on secondhand or even thirdhand information, these guilty managers may have to view the world directly. In times of rapid change, that view can be shocking to people who have avoided it for a long time.

8

Tapping into the Knowledge Net

Cashing in on the art of listening

Intelligence is sufficient to manipulate properly one sector of a larger unit, whether it is a machine or a state. But reason can develop only if it is geared to the whole, if it deals with observable and manageable entities.

ERICH FROMM

A great deal of management alienation can be laid at the feet of two often-conflicting charters given each person involved: (1) to detect the need for change and (2) to implement that change. Until now, the treatment of these responsibilities in business has been unquestionably one-sided: we constantly emphasize management *power* and overlook management *perception*. To manage in change, this imbalance needs correcting. We must not only pay attention to what we *do*; we must give equal regard to *how we decide* what we *should do*. This is where the skill of listening comes in. Although many companies may only pay lip service to the notion of better listening, a surprising number are actively pursuing and nurturing this critical skill.

The signals that hint at an increased interest in the art of listening fill the business community. Some are product-oriented and tangible, while others simply involve greater emphasis on listening skills and less emphasis on telemetry. Here are some of them.

Signposts of Change

- **More surveys, questionnaires, and market tests.** Under changing conditions, information is at once the least expensive and the most valuable resource a company can obtain.

- **Managers asking more questions, more often, of more people.** If we want to know what's happening and why, we must ask the people who are making it happen. A manager in change asks more and orders less.

- **More frequent studies, analyses, pilot programs.** As the prices and penalties of commitment expand, the knowledge that must precede commitment becomes more critical.

- **Preponderance of external and internal audits.** More participants, more alternatives, more risks, and a greater insistence on prudence give rise to more audits. Audits follow change as certainly as day follows night.

- **More management participation in nonwork networks (clubs, charities, teams, societies, etc.).** To listen more, we need to listen in different circles. Networks outside the company often reveal more than the communication channels within it.

- **"Listening training" for executives.** Most managers succeed by making things happen. Considering businesschange, though, what we make happen and how we make it happen are functions of how well we listen. Listening is a skill that must be taught and learned.

- **More formalized debriefings of failures and successes.** There are many subtle lessons among our failures and our successes, and they often lie begging for our attention. The constant readjustment demanded by change requires that we heed these lessons.

- **More frequent communication with noncompetitive firms.** We are not alone, nor is every other company a competitor. It is in our mutual interest to share information with similar firms in similar circumstances.

- **Management retreats, outings, and "ponder meetings."** Another neglected management skill is *thinking*, or more precisely, *pondering*. We need to stop our constant information processing and tune our thinking skills. This won't happen unless we force it.

- **Worker participation in innovation and problem solving (quality circles).** Production workers are no longer being viewed as "tools with two feet." If we are to survive in change, we can no longer ignore their sentient contribution. "Avoidable waste is treating 'human capital' as having all muscle and no mind, forfeiting the inventory of ideas possessed by labor" (Green & Berry, 1985, p. 286).

Comprehension and Control

If the world around us remained stationary, the only changes would be those which we induced. The only movement taking place would be among those things that we pushed. In the past, when things were less inclined to change on their own, we could focus our management attention on whatever we manipulated, watching to see how our management effect took place. In times of change, however, things are apt to move without our intervention or with motion not anticipated by us. To heighten our response to change, we can no longer afford such selective perception.

A primary lesson taught by change is that we cannot go on considering only that which we push, squeeze, or otherwise manipulate. Our vision and hearing must expand, so that we may detect movement not of our doing: incurred as well as induced change, along with all the unwanted or unexpected noise and penalties our own activity initiates. More of our attention will be needed on the *comprehension* segment of the management loop—at the expense of our fascination with the *control* side. We must listen more and manipulate less.

This chapter explores the ways this new shift in consciousness can take place. We shall examine the notion of business "listening" as it pertains to change by expanding the concept of perception. Expanding perception requires an ability to detect change indirectly, intuitively, and outside or tangential to our limited business realms. In expanding our perception, we will discover that change-directed listening is much broader, sensitive to much more, and a great deal more revealing than the kind of listening embodied in the mere *measuring* that would suffice in a static environment.

To survive under dynamic conditions, we must be able to detect more than *differences*. We must be able to detect *motion*, and we must develop an ever-current knowledge of movement as it continually occurs. We must appreciate and be able to track dynamic differences either before or soon after they unfold. There is no magic or special talent required to listen for change and appreciate its presence. All we need is an attentive attitude, broad interests, and a few practiced skills. To attain these prerequisites to management in change, however, we must first recognize both the power that listening brings to the listener and the importance of listening in business management.

Because our abilities to perceive and manage in change are limited by us, we must destroy those artificial limitations that have no benefit in the business experience of today and tomorrow. Chief among these are limitations that restrict our ability to listen, to extract meaning from the overwhelming waves of data that assault or evade our senses daily, and to put that meaning to work.

Listening as a Management Concept

So far, in developing our discussion of the phenomenon of change, we have used the concept of vision in various metaphors to describe the difficulty and error associated with perception. We have mentioned fixed-focus lenses, depth perception, peripheral vision, and the like. These analogies make sense in describing the active, *directed* watching of or looking at something. When we expand our concept of perception, however, we must find a way to sense *without direction*, without focus or discrimination among the objects of our effort. Rather than point at and target that which we wish to "see," we must also spread a far-reaching net outward in all directions, the better to sense without pointing: the better to *listen*.

"Listening" is a far more appropriate word than is "seeing" to indicate a receptiveness to changing conditions and events. We can listen for sounds from all directions and from all distances, without having to filter out any. Sight, on the other hand, seems to correspond well with only one element of perception: sharply focused, directed, and planned perception. As such, the concept of *looking* fits perception of induced change— change which we can plan and the results of which we can measure. We have a pretty good idea how, when, and where induced change will occur, and we can therefore design and construct our management scaffolding to give us the best view of it. None of this is true for incurred change—change that we don't plan and don't foresee, change the source, strength, and duration of which we cannot pinpoint.

Small Investment, Big Payoff

Just as we can think of *looking* as a figurative arrow pointing from the viewer to the object, we can consider *listening* as a circular net surrounding the listener and radiating into infinity in all directions. While looking is more precise and directed, it is also much more expensive and deliberate. In order to see, we must select direction and distance and adjust each as our object adjusts (changes). Hearing requires no such effort. We simply let our ears receive whatever signals happen to come along. Hearing businesschange is less expensive than seeing it. All we need is a receptive attitude, once the threads of our figurative web start to twitch and vibrate.

To profit through change we need to develop a receptive frame of mind and tune our listening skills. The rest is analysis. We must capture and analyze whatever sounds impinge on our listening nets. We must determine, if we can, their strength, origin, pattern, trends, permanence, dilation or contraction, and float. All these "sound characteristics" are actually "change characteristics." This makes listening an apt metaphor for the real-life task of change perception and recognition, because although we can select which variable to manipulate, we can never select what is available to be heard. Then too, we can never predict the area in which the activity of listening will yield managerially significant results.

Finally, if we look around the world at companies and cultures that have developed the skill of listening to high levels, we will see some outstanding commercial enterprises. The Japanese example is unavoidable. What all those thousands of Japanese businessmen and engineers were doing as they toured the many factories, mines, farms, and offices that would open their gates in the 1950s, 1960s and 1970s was plain and simple: they were *listening*. They were gleaning information; listening to what we had and how we thought, as a prerequisite to developing something *better*. We need only consider the deluge of better and lower-priced Japanese products that fill every shop and showroom in the free world to understand the power of an economy fueled by information and practiced in the art of listening.

Which Way Is the Giant Headed?

Closer to home we find the story of IBM and its impact on personal computers and software. A late entry to the PC field, IBM seemed to be waiting and watching at the beginning of the desktop revolution. Other more "entrepreneurial" companies such as Apple, Commodore, and Texas Instruments beat this giant to the marketplace and captured tremendous market share. These machines relied on the C/PM operating system, which was developed by Digital Research, Inc., and is well suited to the needs of small-capacity microprocessors. As the only standard, most software houses and hardware suppliers adapted C/PM in their products. All the while IBM waited, poised on the edge of a vast market they were sure to invade, sooner or later. During this time, other astute firms geared up to listen, and held design and manufacturing commitments in abeyance. They were waiting for the inevitable—the IBM PC.

No one expected price cutting by the giant. What IBM is known for is its size, standing, and reputation as the standard-bearer of the information industry. The months leading up to the IBM PC announcement were electric with tension and speculation. The others waited not to see what the product would look like or sell for, but what new "standards" it would embody. They listened to hear which way the giant was headed.

As expected, IBM introduced a totally new (and of course, incompatible) operating system of its own: the MS/DOS system. Once this was known, hardware and software firms by the thousands scrambled to accommodate it—to convert their products and ideas to the new standard. Those who detected this change soonest had a head start. In an industry begging for standards, IBM stepped in and provided them. The rest followed their lead. And before they did it, a thousand ears were pressed to the ground as every company in the field listened for the giant's footsteps.

In contrast, when SONY introduced its Betamax videocassette recorder (VCR), many firms expected it to be the upcoming standard. Thousands of films were produced in the Beta format. Those that waited and listened, however, soon discovered that JVC Corporation had patented a new VHS format and licensed it to many other manufacturers. Listeners found that the price of VHS-type VCR's was about to plunge as a result of these new entries into what had been a SONY-dominated market. Hence, the VHS format became the standard, and those who sensed this trend early enough benefited by it. In this case, listening to the giant didn't pay off—one needed to hear the sounds of the herd instead.

A Prerequisite to the Management Effect

The concept of management most often seen in the past held that managing was composed of two sequential elements: (1) *planning*, by which we decide what we want to affect, and (2) *controlling*, by which we ensure our effect is gained. Good managers planned their work well and followed through by monitoring, measuring, and directing so that they could control events and circumstances to meet that plan. While essential to induced change, planning and controlling are not sufficient for mastering all change. Both incurred change and the unwanted noise and penalties of induced change are ignored by the functions of planning and controlling. Something else is needed: an ability to account for the rest of the phenomenon. This is only achieved through listening.

If planning and controlling concern those elements of change we want to bring about, *recognizing* and *accommodation* are their counterparts for those other elements which we neither plan nor control, expect nor determine.

We should never be so self-aggrandizing as to believe we can plan and control all managerially significant events or circumstances, or to think that nothing moves unless we push it. The world moves without our encouragement, and often despite it—despite our best plans and most careful controls. We need an ability to recognize and accommodate this unharnessed change in a manner consistent with our expectations and processes. We need to build and use the overlooked link in our perception loop. We need to listen.

With induced as well as incurred change, the ability to perceive always precedes the ability to direct or accommodate (to profit). If our management function is composed of these two loops, perception is a prerequisite for direction. We enhance perception by selecting directed *vision* and by hearing unselected *sounds* of change. Vision requires extensive scaffolding, planning, and preparation, while listening requires little more than attitude. Both are necessary, for we can never presume to control that which we do not plan nor to accommodate that which we do not recognize.

The Forest of Change

Predatory mammals tend to have forward-mounted eyes and forward-directed vision—the better to concentrate on pursuit of one selected object, their prey. Their potential victims need quite different vision—that allowing detection of unselected objects. These animals have eyes mounted on the sides of their head and vision that is less focused but more expansive. They need to detect motion before they can direct attention to it. To be effective in change, we need both types of vision, but so far it seems we've assumed the directed sense to be more important. In the forest of change, though, we are more apt to be prey than predator. We need one eye from the fox and another from the hare.

The Increasing Value of Information

That abundant and available information is exploding upon every business scene is no news to anyone in commerce, education, industry, or government. Information impinges upon us from all directions, with all sorts of intensity and urgency, and in all manners imaginable. Never before has management been so well endowed with information or so well equipped to receive, transmit, and transduce it. Never has so much information been moving so rapidly in so many directions as at present. And this abundance shows signs of increasing well into the future. The manager of today and tomorrow is swimming in information.

Just because there is so much more information and we are so much better equipped to process it doesn't mean that information is that much better or more important than in the past. Abundance and versatility never have led, by themselves, to increased value. To the contrary, surplus often lowers value, or at least price. Why is it, then, that with so much information and so much information-processing capability at our command the *value* of information has continued to increase? Why do we treasure information more than ever before?

The answer lies in the increasing influence of change in our business world. Information is the key to the planning, control, recognition, and accommodation of change. Information defines change and relates its meaning to us. It reveals the presence, action, and character of dynamic difference. Information *announces* change. Sometimes the announcement is in the form of a clarion call impossible to ignore, but at other times it is no more than a whisper, hinting at subtlety and suggesting nuance. To manage in change we need to become more attentive not only to the blasts but to the whispers.

The Evolution of Perception

It pays to understand the different stages of perception as they pertain to both control and accommodation of change. To begin, all knowledge starts with raw data. These may be in the form of facts, laws, constraints, or simple numbers signifying dimension or quantity. Data are transformed into information by us, by our interpretation and understanding of their structure, content, and texture. But simply having information does us little good. We need to change information to understanding, to *meaning*. Once meaning is attained, we are in a position to use information for the betterment of ourselves and our business functions.

Computers and software never provide information or meaning; they simply process data in a fashion that increases its availability and amenability to change. Humans provide this change by applying their experience, knowledge, and wisdom. We alone can transform data into information and information into meaning.

As people in a corporation progress from production tasks to management positions, their ability to make this transformation becomes more and more important. Production workers need data; they need to know "what" is to be done and even "how" to do it. Managers, on the other hand, need to know much more; they need to know "why" something must be done and why alternatives to doing it are not wise. The evolution of a business person from production to management levels is parallel to the evolution of data from raw material to articulated meaning.

Every electrician will tell us that it takes a much larger, stronger, and more expensive cable to transmit power than to receive or transmit information. Another sort of power can be seen on the manipulation side of the management effect, the link between what we want to achieve and what we do achieve. Power and control go hand in hand, with control being the intelligence that wields and directs power. On the reception side of the management loop, less expensive "wire" is needed to pick up and receive data, information, or knowledge. In the field of business management, it takes less effort, money, and time to erect the apparatus of knowledge than the apparatus of power. Unfortunately, however, too much emphasis has been traditionally placed on the power side of the function, on what one *does* rather than how one *determines what to do*. The difference between a decider and a doer, however, is what separates management from production. In the business world there are many who can do, but few who can decide. To achieve management prowess we must recognize this difference and choose to exercise and strengthen our decision skills. The key to this effort is an ability to perceive, to listen, and to watch. The finely woven network of "information wire" that surrounds an effective manager in change is just as important as, albeit more fragile and less forceful than, the few large, direct cables of power emanating from that manager.

Targeting Our Effect

Information, properly transformed to meaning, is the magic of management in times of change. A well-informed manager hears but disobeys the advice to "shoot first and ask questions later." This manager realizes that every company has only so much ammunition, only so many guns, and only a limited amount of time to fire them, especially when the targets are whizzing all about, constantly in motion and constantly in flux. Information allows us to practice careful aim and select just the right targets of opportunity, becoming sharpshooters with high-powered rifles rather than harried defenders of the status quo blasting away with shotguns at whatever moves.

By listening better we are able to receive much more of the valuable information that is available, and to receive it much more rapidly and at greatly reduced cost. We can anticipate certain effects and changes, and can prepare to control or accommodate them once they are upon us. We can then turn our antennae toward change, much as we focus our control mechanisms on desired effects. We can determine which effect is needed and which effects are not needed. We can discriminate, we can decide.

The unplanned management effect is as empty as activity without process contribution, motion without purpose—squirrels in a cage. An intelligently planned effect is based on a manager's knowledge of *why* something should be done (or avoided). This is what separates management from rote performance; in which only a knowledge of *how* is important.

Listening on Different Levels

The ways we listen are often indicative of our reasons for listening, and these vary with our respective roles in any business organization. At the first and most basic level are those who need to know how to do something. These are the *performers*, who are involved in the process links of our business. They are often directed by the *supervisors*, who need to know what needs to be done. Above the supervisors are the *managers*, who should know why what is being done is necessary.

In times of fixed constants we could stop here, having built a simple model of a generic company organization: the performers, the supervisors, and the managers, each with a different reason for listening. But when change is considered as the greatest challenge to business, another level is necessary. This level consists of those who need to know not only what to do, how to do it, and why it must be done but *what makes it preferable to other actions*. This upper level is populated by managers who thrive in change—deciders, listeners, whose actions are tempered by knowledge of all alternatives and appreciation of the power of articulated change and the danger of change that is unaccommodated. Listening helps them separate what is preferable from the universe of what is possible.

Listening requires receptivity to signals, while manipulating requires transmission of directed force. Listening uses our business nerve system, while manipulating uses our muscles. Subtle differences also exist. For one, listening doesn't require much of a commitment of resources or effort—just an attitude. Manipulation requires time, money, people, and material, and it requires a commitment of these factors before it can begin. Manipulation demands a selection, a decision about what and how to manipulate, and a mobilization of force to bring it about. Listening requires none of these. It is a much less demanding, less extractive exercise. In fact, listening sometimes allows us to profit without manipulating at all. If we hear of an opportunity, we can sometimes exploit it simply by knowing about it, without changing it in any way. It is, as the saying goes, much easier to ride a train in the direction it is going. Listening lets us do this. It is a skill that begs for enhancement.

Ways to Enhance Listening

Of the many ways to enhance our ability to listen and reap the bountiful rewards it brings, most can be classified into two groups: (1) additudinal and (2) technique. Additudinal improvements are easier to make and yield the greatest incremental benefit. Once each company or manager has the proper attitude regarding the place listening holds in our skill inventory, the improvements made by advanced technique are available. What follows is a collection of techniques and attitudinal adjustments that help business leaders listen better.

1. *Admit the criticality of listening.* This admission precedes any benefit one can obtain. Before any listening apparatus or technique can be meaningfully developed, we need to recognize that listening is an essential element of the management function, and not a sideline, hobby, or ancillary task. A bit of management humility goes a long way toward enhancing the listening skill. The most successful managers in change realize they aren't the most intelligent, they don't have all the answers, and they can learn by listening to events and to others.

2. *Tap into existing nets.* Most businesses are surrounded by organized networks consisting of individuals with common interests and by existing nets of information extending from each individual or group. Since both these fabrics exist on their own, the wise manager knows they can yield extensive information without much creative expense. Tapping into networks or information nets is much like tapping into telephone lines designed and constructed by others. All we need to do is plug into them and listen. The information is virtually free.

In describing the emerging networking phenomenon, Naisbitt emphasizes this powerful ability. He writes: "One of networking's great attractions is that it is an easy way to get information. ... Although sharing information and contacts is their main purpose, networks can go beyond the mere transfer of data to the creation and exchange of knowledge" (1982, p. 194).

3. *Search for dimensional information.*   Listening carefully and over a period of time, from many vantage points and with learning as a goal, we are able to determine much more about a signal than merely its direction and strength. Skilled listeners seek a pattern, trends, relationships, differences, and other sound dimensions. We don't listen simply to ascertain data, but to derive meaning, and meaning is attained when we understand the features, texture, tone, shape, and configuration of whatever sends the signals. Meaning is to data as music is to noise. By searching for dimensional information we attempt to derive meaning from the listening experience.

4. *Listen to variables not manipulated.*   A common management tendency is to observe what we push very carefully while ignoring the rest of the world. We focus on the manipulated variable and shut out the rest. Unfortunately, the rest of the world changes on its own, or with little regard for our intervention. In order to understand change we must listen to all sounds, not just the ones we cause.

5. *Listen to change targets.*   Change targets often give us very early indications of the nature of change and its potential effects on our businesses. Change targets are similar to lightning rods, attracting change and drawing its power down upon us. As our change targets are impacted first, they serve to warn us. We then need to jettison whatever is of like nature.

6. *Avoid sensitivity ruts.*   When we listen only for certain sounds of change, our ability to detect the rest becomes atrophied or numb. Our sensitivity diminishes to a point at which it is responsive only to selected stimuli. We live in sensitivity ruts when we talk to only a select few of our peers or superiors, when we deal only with people within the company, when we ignore the actions of companies not in the same industry or geographic area as ourselves.

A general rule is that the higher up people climb in management, the less often they can afford to sink into a listening rut. Unfortunately, it often seems that the higher most managers go, the deeper their rut becomes; they become isolated, insulated, and unaware of storms of change raging all about them.

The danger of such an attitude has always been apparent to astute management. In *The New Competitors*, D. Quinn Mills tells us, "Only if change is seen as a top down process are top managers hypocritical to encourage participative management for others while remaining autocratic themselves. In fact, participative elements have always drawn their long range strength and energy from the shop floor" (1985, p. 355).

7. *Visit other cultures.*   It is difficult to listen for what one has never heard of or thought about. Each personal environment or business culture is unique and involves only a few dimensions of experience and information. Much can be learned, and our listening skills improved, by experiencing life outside our specific business environments, among cultures unfamiliar and exotic.

8. *Find your identity.*   You listen better when you know who and where you are. People lost in a search for their personal or corporate identity cannot turn their attention outward and receive information from others. Our company's identity is the starting point for detection of significant differences among ourselves and others. If we don't understand our unique distinctions in the business community, we cannot distinguish sharp contrasts or differences of either a static or a dynamic nature.

Not only should we know what and where we are at all times, but we should find out why these factors have sometimes been insufficient. We should find out why we fail, lose sales, miss contracts, aren't selected for award, and the like. The answers to these questions are the most valuable information any company may receive. It usually takes little analysis to transform the lessons of "why we failed" into "how we can succeed."

9. *Use the mirror.*   This technique involves honest self-appraisal—listening to or judging ourselves. Since our perspective is unique, any lessons it brings are unique and may be suspect or tainted. When we hold up a mirror to ourselves and ask for comments, we gain the benefit of vastly different perspectives. The best impressions we often get are the surprises, the ones we didn't expect but that, once gained, are very enlightening. Progressive companies survive change because they have a grip on their individual affective essence. This understanding is easiest to obtain by looking from the outside inward, a view many managements never seek or get.

10. *Listen to pain.*   "Business pain" is another term for "bad news." Examples are the objections customers bring us. Many companies meet customer objections with counterobjections: "Our product failed because you didn't follow the directions," "Our delivery was late because you issued an erroneous purchase order," or "Our construction failed because your design was faulty." Others simply refuse to acknowledge the basis for any objection or turn a deaf ear to it. Neither approach is recommended.

The best approach to objections, in times of change or not, is to defuse the anger and animosity around the objection and to make an honest attempt to understand it. This means we must listen to objectors. If an objection is without merit, merely listening to it will defuse its damaging effects. If it has merit we will benefit from understanding it and learning how to prevent similar mistakes. It is stupid to consider objections stupid, even though many are.

What Hampers Listening

We often learn from negative examples just as forcefully as from positive ones. This is true of the skill of listening. For every useful technique or proper listening attitude, there are erroneous counterparts. It is beneficial to recognize the attitudes and techniques that hamper listening in order to arrange for their suppression or removal. Here are the most common ones.

1. *A management bias toward action.* Undue emphasis on doing, on motion, on effect no matter how wisely selected or attained, diminishes the importance of listening as a management function. If we insist on measuring direct effects, tying causes to them, and discounting the indirect and tangential or latent benefits of listening, we will drive the value of listening to artificial lows. Listening is like nurturing in this regard. It is a facilitative attitude and a contributing approach rather than a direct manipulation of the environment for which a measurable increment of benefit can be determined. Companies that reward only action drive their managements to value gross activity over targeted intervention, motion over progress, and the power of direct shock over the more effective action of subtlety. A management bias toward raw action is often a bias away from articulated, well-conceived, and intelligent action—a bias away from listening.

2. *Management hubris.* Management which considers itself omniscient places little value on the benefits of listening, no matter how easily or inexpensively they may be obtained. Self-satisfied managers see little need for improvement and therefore have little regard for listening. They see truth as something reserved for their exclusive discovery—often as a result of their manipulation. This attitude relegates listening to simple buzzword status rather than elevating it to the essential management art it should be.

3. *Undue emphasis on the numbers.* Managements suffering from this tendency do not "see" anything but weights and measures. They are

insensitive to all but quantifiable or unitized differences. Unfortunately, they fail to realize that life has its own ways of expressing differences and that these outnumber our limited dimensions of quantification. Undue emphasis on the quantitative effect of information neglects many of its most important aspects. Subtlety, nuance, tone, texture, alignment, beauty, fear, pride, concern, and inevitability: which numbering scheme fully defines these?

4. *Obsession with the optimum.* The continuous pursuit of perfection in one aspect of business leads to neglect of its other aspects. Optimization shuts out diversification. Its focus is narrow and its benefits incremental, at best. Beyond a certain point, we serve our effort better by looking and listening in all directions, by surveying the full 360 degrees of our position rather than delving deeper and deeper into one aspect. Infatuation with the optimum places blinders on our vision, filters on our hearing. It excludes knowledge of or consideration of alternatives.

5. *Being unilingual or unicultural.* If exposure to and appreciation of other cultures or other meanings enhances listening, then those of us who speak only one "language" or recognize only one culture are severely handicapped listeners. This means that executives who have spent their entire careers with one company or even in one industry may be incomplete listeners, just as restricted in outlook and perception as those who have dwelt for extended periods of time in one speciality box.

In times of change, when we say that a manager "knows the 'company way' inside and out" we may be criticizing rather than complimenting. Those who know the company way are sometimes so hard-wired in their attitudes and techniques, not to mention their receptiveness, that they can't recognize valid patterns coming from elsewhere. If we listen to one song over and over again, we learn that song quite well. We may even go so far as to presume that this song alone constitutes the entire universe of music, and that others are simply noise. When this happens, the unilingual or unicultural manager can be pronounced "brain-dead."

6. *Having no time to ponder.* Today's managers spend a lot of time processing data, manipulating, planning, and measuring. They are often too busy "doing" to have time to stop, to look, to "listen." Time spent listening and pondering is valuable because it allows one to break away from mental ties to process functions and lets the true management perspective unfold. We all need more time to consider, to think, to ponder what lies all about us, and to structure meaning and relevance to our work experiences beyond that given by mere motion or activity. To ignore this need is to condemn managers to lives as squirrels in cages, always running but never understanding where it gets them.

Listening includes appreciating and experiencing, as well as considering what, why, and why not. This is why we call it an "experience" and not a "process." We listen best when we stop doing, when all our perceptive and intuitive powers are trained on the experience—when we create the time and the opportunity to ponder. No machine, process, scaffolding, or exotic management fad can substitute for this experience. It is strictly a human one, rare and to be treasured.

7. *Dedication to scaffolding.* If we've spent a great deal of time and money building information and control networks, we may become devoted to their exclusive use, to the detriment of listening. This attitude can be expressed as follows: "If it doesn't come through my sophisticated telemetry, it doesn't exist or is of no importance." When our perception apparatus dominates, our ability to perceive becomes as restrictive as dedication to capital investment is to our changing business needs. Many companies are guilty of excessive *information investments* as well as excessive capital *conversion investments.*

8. *Polarization.* Polarization is the process of dividing the universe of possibility into two distinct camps. Polarized views consider the world as being either black or white, hot or cold, friend or foe, right or wrong. If we listen with this extreme bias, we either (1) don't hear all the thousands of shades of gray in between the black and white notes or (2) artificially transform all received signals into one of the two camps we have in mind.

Surveys, questionnaires, and sampling exercises do this quite often. If our company information nets pick up only that which hurts or that which helps the company, we won't get much information at all. Most information is neutral or latent in impact. In a world of change, it's very important to detect this neutral or latent information and to watch for its movement. It may migrate to the hurtful or the helpful camp at a moment's notice.

Developing Contrasts

Every manager, whether in change or not, needs to both listen and manipulate. These activities must be in balance; however, oftentimes we see managers biased toward one side or the other of the management effect, toward listening or manipulating. Aligned with the notion of synthesis used throughout this analysis is the need to synthesize both elements of the management function, to blend the art of listening with the skill of manipulation. A polarization toward one or the other is dangerous.

We seldom see extreme polarization, rarely find either a totally insensitive manager doing the work with a bludgeon or a totally pensive, do-nothing listener. But we do see gradations, managers who lean toward either perception or direction. Let's contrast these two inclinations.

A Manipulating Manager:	*A Listening Manager:*
Likes to push.	Prefers to pull.
Knows what is done.	Knows what "doing" accomplishes.
Looks to walk down a path.	Listens to choose a path.
Lists the features of rustling leaves.	Hears leaves rustle.
Is in awe of data speed and quantity.	Sifts through data to glean meaning.
Implements what has been chosen.	Chooses what is to be implemented.
Cherishes power tools.	Cherishes precision tools.
Knows what is in front of him or her.	Knows what he or she is in the presence of.

The Prices and Risks of Listening More and Manipulating Less

Without sensible construction and tempered application, many of the suggestions expressed or implied here can be taken erroneously or used inappropriately. We need to mention a few of the prices and risks of a bias toward listening and away from manipulating in the management function, in order to round out our discussion of this business response to change.

The greatest risk a company faces in listening more is that little action will take place—that *too much* study, analysis, and other forms of listening will occur. Without question, we cannot become a company of listeners who don't also perform, plan, control, and accommodate. Listening needs its fair share of attention as a valued management skill, but no more than its fair share. Infatuation with listening often leads to inability to act, to assume risks, and to gain results.

To be good listeners, we must be open to everything, not just to invited information. This means we will hear bad news along with the good, criticism as well as compliments. To managers averse to hearing criticism; listening can be quite painful. When we listen carefully, we cannot escape the sounds of our own faults and inadequacies.

Listening stimulates thinking, pondering, and consideration of things not presented by rote activity, by process functions. To those who find comfort in mindless work, in performance of "no-brainers," listening can be difficult and uncomfortable.

Listening also produces scant direct, measurable results against which we can balance its minor costs. Its results are subtle, latent, or tangential to our tabulations. Like nurturing, listening produces few direct, traceable products. This by no means diminishes its value. It simply expresses the difficulty we have with quantifying the results of listening. Listening produces few "squeaks per tweak."

Listening also requires a certain ability to transcend, to penetrate barriers within or around our company or group boundaries, and to expose ourselves to different cultures in order to become fully developed. This generalization of perception is consistent with other generalizing pressures brought about by change, and is another reason to slow down the march of specialization within our businesses.

To listen without responding to what we hear makes us fascinated spectators of the business world rather than active participants. If we listen too much and manipulate too little, we remove ourselves from the business experience. Each of us, no matter the nature of our business or the extent of our management charter, must be held ultimately responsible for results. The art of listening doesn't make results any more expensive to attain, however. It simply makes us cognizant of change and able to bring about results in a more articulated, better-directed, and more intelligent manner.

9

Working with Pulses, Not Streams

Using projects to capture opportunity

Only to a magician is the world forever fluid,
infinitely mutable and eternally new. Only he
knows truly that all things are crouched in
eagerness to become something else, and it is
from this universal tension that he draws his
power.

PETER BEAGLE

Every business response to change presented so far is acting to dramatically transform our concepts of work, of what we do and how we do it. The phenomenon of change has revised our view of business activity, destroyed the viability of accepted business models, and led to new definitions of ourselves and our effect. Although our products or our services may be similar to those of the past, how we bring them about and how reliable that effect can be are no longer taken for granted. A greater understanding and more intelligent response to change forces us to reconsider the very foundations of our work, our contribution to it, and its place in the realm of business. Change is reshaping the nature and meaning of work.

Nowhere is this more pronounced than through the "projectization" of work, its centering in unique, temporary packets of effort. Whereas industrial production and all its social and cultural spin-offs relied upon linear, sequential arrays of highly specialized and synchronized effort (i.e., the automobile assembly line), this new, change-directed concept of work involves parallel, unsynchronized, and generalized effort not tied to or dependent upon any established tools or techniques.

If the concept of work dominant in the past has been symbolized by a *line*, the new representation of work is more apt to be a *circle*—a circle that encloses a comprehensive interaction of concurrent, temporary, and accomplishment-oriented tasks. If the old term for work was "operations," the new term is "projects."

In times of change the project orientation dominates all operational frameworks. The logic supporting this conclusion is inescapable, and we see it manifested with great frequency by business examples all about us. Perceptive managers know, then, that in times of change, for today and tomorrow, they will more often than not be managing *projects*.

We cannot simply count the growing number of efforts our companies now designate as "projects" and hold this increase up as the sole result of a projectization phenomenon. Much more is happening to change the nature of our work and our perception of our role in it. Subtle, project-influenced changes are even taking place in operational settings. Most of all, operationally oriented managers are beginning to understand the unique aspects and conditions of project assignments. Here are some other signposts indicating a widespread turn toward projects.

Signposts of Change

- **Adaptation of the "project manager" designation.** Once regarded as an organizational oddity, the project manager is now invading even the most non-project-oriented companies. In a future dominated by change, every manager, at one time or another, will be a project manager.

- **More temporary, results-directed organizations.** The days of the concrete, tiered organization are gone. We now view all organizations as temporary, goal-directed contrivances—necessary evils rather than structures of intrinsic beauty. Projects cannot be managed by pyramids. They demand clusters of people gathered around a challenge.

- **More common use of outsiders, (consultants, subcontractors, joint ventures, temporaries, etc.) for specific efforts.** Organizations are being built and destroyed on the bases of risk and pragmatism. The old notions of insiders and outsiders don't fit anymore. We'll use whichever players we need, regardless of what uniforms they wear.

- **More local and perishable procedures, plans, standards.** Standards don't work well in times of flux. Like organizations, they will be disposable, situationally responsive, and full of room for discretion.

- **Emphasis on "people skills" among management.** Project management is, first, people management. To coalesce disparate interests, transcend goal conflicts, and create binding mutuality, we will need those who hold people skills.

- **Constant creation and dismantling of management scaffolding.** Procedures, policies, reports, information systems, and progress measurements are all elements of managerial scaffolding. When everything remains static, the scaffolding can be built of steel and anchored in bedrock. In times of change, it must be as temporary and mobile as a tent.

- **Devaluation of tradition, of "what worked last time."** In the world of projects, there simply is no "last time." This is the world of change—the phenomenon that mocks the past. "Avoidable waste is a swelling bureaucracy that produces risk-averse executives who say 'But we've always done it that way' " (Green & Berry, 1985, p. 14).

- **The emergence of pragmatism and resourcefulness over perfection and compliance as favorable management attributes.** We will need scroungers, tinkerers, masters of the extemporaneous, and those who can make it happen, regardless of the rules, the odds, or the inevitable second guess. Project positions are contribution-based and need-justified. Our position and authority will be functions of what we *are doing*, not what we *have done* or *who we are*.

Illustrating the Distinctions*

One must clearly understand and fully appreciate the bold and fine differences between *operations* and *projects* in order to comprehend the powerful influence of change on business. By shifting our needs from operationally achieved work to work accomplished through projects, change has exerted one of its most observable and profound effects. Its impacts reach our notion of work itself, our roles in work, the needs and limitations of management—affecting both our senses of identity and our value systems.

---

*In this chapter I draw from some distinctions made in my earlier book, *Winning at Project Management: What Works, What Fails, and Why* (Wiley, New York, 1986), not to identify all project aspects but to present only those that illustrate business responses to change.

As we draw and give examples of some of the many distinctions between these two approaches to work, we will not only be depicting differences in work orientations but also describing the particular nature and far-reaching impact of change. To understand the differences between operations and projects is to understand the differences between a changeless and a changing world—that is, to understand change itself.

Why Operations and Projects Differ

There are countless differences between operations and projects as ways to organize and manage business effort, and they include concept, context, intent, and application. Rather than defining each and every difference, our approach will be to point out the most significant differences and those which most directly illustrate the effects of change.

Operations are based on the concept of *using* existing systems, properties, processes, and capabilities in a continuous, fairly repetitive fashion. If our business is automobile production, our operational base is composed of physical plant (the factory), tools, equipment, information and control systems, knowledge, and production skills. Our operational objective is to use this fixed potential as efficiently and effectively as possible. Operations are aimed at making the best use of what exists, over and over again.

Fewer Presumptions

Projects, in contrast to operations, presuppose no fixed tools, techniques, or capability. They seek to create a limited impact through temporary and expedient means. The design and construction of an automobile assembly plant is a good example. As such, this "project" is unique and apart from any other undertaken. We produce one "product," the plant, rather than a series of similar products (the cars that will result from operation of the finished plant). Uniqueness of effort and result are the hallmarks of project situations. Consistency and uniformity are typical of operations.

Operations are geared to maintain and exploit, while projects are conceived to create and make exploitation available. Projects, therefore, typically precede operations in the normal business cycle.

Projects are temporary and expedient exercises, while operations are more sustained and continuous, and therefore more amenable to optimization. Economies of scale help to optimize operations, as do trial and error, but given the temporary and unique world of each project, neither of these approaches is very useful in a project. If a successful operation can be imagined as a continuous, uninterrupted *stream* of effort yielding a predictable collection of similar results, we must view each project as a temporary *pulse* of activity yielding a unique, singular result.

Projects represent, then, one-time-only configurations of resources, people, tools, and management expectations, while operations presuppose continuity of the conversion process well into the future. We seldom consider the end of an operation, but we always consider the end of a project as soon as we conceive of its initiation. We expect projects to be completed, to be finished, and, like cruise missiles, to be self-consuming once their singular purposes have been accomplished. Operations may outlive their results, but projects expire when their result is achieved.

Free Variables and Soft Links

In order to exploit induced change, operations rely on circumstances in which most variables are fixed and the rest are manipulated. Working conditions are fairly constant; we are usually enclosed in a factory, office, or shop; and our resources are of like nature and consistent in appearance and quality. Project work, though, is hostage to many free variables, few of which are presumed to be fixed. The fixing of free variables must take place every time a project is initiated, as when staffs are hired, organizations are created, procedures are adopted, plans are made, and lines of communication are strung. Most of these variables are fixed and already in place by the time operational work begins.

Since synchronization is essential to any effort involving more than one participant, both operations and projects need to meet the challenge of synchronization. They differ in how the challenge is met, though. With operations, the links connecting serial work steps are usually "hard" or mechanical, inherent in the equipment, line, material, or techniques used. If metal must be rolled before stamping, we simply position the rollers in advance of the stamping press in the production line. This is a "hard link," designed into the operation and therefore difficult to avoid or circumvent.

With project work, activity cannot be so easily synchronized. We often must depend on forced, artificial, or human linkage, the so-called soft links that tie otherwise disparate work elements together. Soft links include contract terms and conditions ("All steel shall be rolled before stamping"), written procedures, management inspection, and supervision. Soft links require constant enforcement and monitoring, for they may be easily bypassed or ignored. They are much less dependable as guarantees of synchronicity. Again, with project work less is fixed (or fixable) and less can be taken for granted.

We have already described the tension between process- and product-dominated business approaches and seen how a product-oriented effort better fits changing conditions. This also applies to a project effort, where we begin with an expected set of results and seek to find or build a collection of processes to bring it about (*result drives process*). With operations the reverse is true. We begin with a process (factory, plant, refinery, line, etc.) and search for materials to feed it and markets in which to discharge the result (*process drives product*).

Project work is also amenable to the pressure change exerts toward generalization and away from specialty restrictions. Project work, by its nature, begins with nothing and relies on synthesis to proceed. It requires coalescence: bringing elements together and creating mutuality among them. Operations tend to divide labor and its contribution into discrete, incremental stages. In fact, division of labor is a hallmark of the industrial revolution.

Change Sensitivity or Defiance

Because of their fixed conditions, hard links, stationary components, and hard-wired process steps, most operational efforts are rightly classified as insensitive to change or defiant of it. They shield themselves as much as possible from incurred change and stick to their original goals, methods and results. They typify the *enduring* quality of work, employing the "hardening" we have used to describe change-immune designs (Chapter 3). Project work cannot be so shielded. It is conceived, born, lives, and expires in change. It evolves continuously, because of both induced and incurred change. It takes a different approach to the challenge of change immunity; it opts for disposability or adaptation rather than durability.

Finally, we must recognize that operations take time, money, and a great deal of effort to establish, long before the first product rolls off the end of the line. All the capital investment, design, hard wiring, and variable fixing they employ must precede their use. Once erected, operational apparatus cranks out a great deal of product at lower and lower unit cost. The question is, "Do we have the time to spend and the resources to sink before the first stream of products starts to flow?" Unless we exist in a relatively static environment, the answer is, "No, we have neither."

When conditions are in a state of flux, opportunities are fleeting, and our businesses must seize the moment, the rapid deployment of a project effort is much more suitable. If the targets of opportunity remain similar and stationary for long periods of time, if they are unthreatening and fixed, we can design and erect a very efficient method of shooting them down. This is the operational solution. If instead we are running through a jungle of beasts, some pursued and some pursuing, the ability to quickly access and deploy *any* weapon is much more important to us. Selecting the *available,* albeit not often *ideal,* weapon is the project solution. Changing conditions favor the pragmatic.

The Project Anomaly

Projects are a special type of business anomaly. They often evolve, change shape, and resist definition (as force waves, for example, do), but then again, they are always composed of discrete items such as people, re- sources, and conversion processes (as are particles of mass). And we can never point to, look at, or "see" a project (as we can never see subatomic matter). We can see project activity and results, and we can see project managers and production workers doing their work. But even when considered all together, these factors do not actually make up the project model; they are simply parts of it. Projects follow the concept of *holism* or *synergy* in that each is a "collection of entities or objects that can generate a larger reality not analyzable in terms of the components themselves" (Berman, 1984, p. 353).

The best way to model a project is not to use a visual representation at all. A project is a *mutual effort,* using a collection of resources in an orchestrated way to achieve a joint goal. As such, projects are like "waves"— forces and bundles of energy moving through time—each with its own identity, culture, methods of conversion, and contrived cohesion. Upon accomplishment of the project goal, this contrived cohesion no longer serves to bind the project together (thus making it an anachronism); instead, it dissolves the project—dissipating the project wave upon the beach of success.

It's easy to identify project work in architecture or engineering, for the physical result symbolizes the project effort itself. A new power plant, a factory, a shopping mall, and an aircraft carrier are examples. But the project model applies to many other fields and to efforts most of us are involved with at one time or another. Here is a partial list of other efforts that might fit the definition of "project":

Performing a heart transplant

Designing a new weapons system

Producing a stage play

Developing a strategic business plan

Researching and writing a book

Conducting a political campaign

Renovating an antique automobile

Producing a motion picture

Establishing a small business

Throwing a party

Introducing a new product

Taking a vacation trip

Designing and installing a computer network

Creating an occupational training program

There is a subtle commonality in all these examples. They each involve (1) working with few existing standards, (2) the need for creativity and synthesis, (3) a temporary pulse of effort, and (4) a keen sense of, if not reliance on, the phenomenon of change.

The Direction of Change

Each element characterizing a project, and differentiating it from operations, can be seen as a change-directed quality. Projects are the perfect response to change. They are no less than change-responsive bundles of effort. Because they more closely represent waves, and not incompressible particles, projects can expand; shrink; bend; accelerate and slow down; change shape and direction; and escape the burdens of capitalization, process addiction, and hardness. While operations try to withstand the impacts of change, projects ride along with it: business waves upon the sea of time.

Forces and Factors Favoring Project Orientations

Once we understand the project concept and couple it with what we know about change, it's easy to see why projects are becoming more and more the accepted context of work. Here we should briefly mention why this is true.

Rapid creation and deployment allow project efforts to respond quickly to changed conditions. Their independence from capital burdens lets our work flex with or dodge unforeseen changes in technology or process methodology. The fleeting nature of opportunity gives its rewards only to the most adaptive, mobile pursuer. Project orientations provide that mobility; we can move our effort to the opportunity rather than attempt to entice it into our operating environment, in terms of space and time.

This explains the sudden and successful emergence of *entrepreneurism* in today's business culture. Entrepreneurs succeed where large, static organizations fail—because of their flexibility, mobility, and pursuit. Entrepreneurs are lean and responsive, able to quickly detect and pursue the opportunities that change strews all about. Even with the most expensive, powerful mechanism, a large supertanker needs miles of space and huge amounts of time to execute a complete 180-degree turn, whereas a small speedboat can turn on a dime.

Changing markets, resources, prices, and needs do not allow us the benefit of time or of the fixed variables that operations presuppose. Project work is amendable to dynamic conditions, while operations demand static ones. The tendency of change to emphasize purpose over process (Chapter 4) also runs counter to the operational premise (process in search of purpose) and diminishes the value of pursuing process enhancements.

If change serves to make any given method or technique less lasting and more perishable, then it also devalues fixed versions of processes and operations. If an operation is dependent on technique and that technique is made obsolete through change, the operation becomes obsolete. Project work has few dependencies, and those it suffers are seldom exclusive.

The Contribution of Business Megachange

Megachanges in the business world itself, each caused partly by recognition of the power of change, also seem to be running in the project direction. These are (1) *variation* in enterprise among megacompanies, (2) *diversification* of risk and assets, (3) use of more *distributed* information and effort (outsourcing, subcontracting, joint ventures, prefabrication elsewhere, containerization, process packaging, etc.), and (4) *decentralization* of business authority and management effect.

Each of these megachanges should have had and has had a tremendous effect on our reevaluation of work and how we relate to it. And each favors the project orientation. Whether they are effects of change or causes of change itself, they signal a new business culture, more cognizant of and more responsive to change. If we are going to manage in the future, we are going to have to manage in this culture—this culture which is impacted by change and in which work is more often than not "projectized."

The New Business Culture

The emergence and proliferation of the project model of work, of work as integrated pulses rather than a continuous line, is helping to define a new and very different business culture. This culture will be dominated by a need to generalize, to spread awareness and ability over large spaces and times, rather than to focus both on ever-narrowing fields of specialty. If generalization represents the prevailing condition of the new business culture, then *synthesis* represents the activity that will bring it about. The ability to synthesize—to coalesce or bring together the forces and resources needed to equip a project effort—is quickly becoming the critical ability of the future. "Synthesis" and "adaptation" are fast replacing "optimization" as the watchwords of today's management.

Management in change will more often be judged by its results than by its inherent sophistication, complexity, or level of detail. A business culture ruled by pragmatism will tend to value accomplishment over refinement, attainment of goals over perfection of a limited ability to attain them. To be truly adaptive, we will embrace independence of any certain set of plans, tools, techniques, or conversion processes. We will view such factors as simply means to an end, and means of temporary and utilitarian value. No business will transcend time and change totally intact, for no business is immune to these forces.

If we are to adapt, our methods and scaffolding must be malleable, disposable, and expedient. We can no longer shackle our companies to any given feature, no matter how well it has served us in the past nor how attached or dependent upon it our managers have become. Managers in change are independent managers, serving not technique or tool but higher principles which do transcend momentary changes. These principles are pragmatism, expediency, reason, adaptability, independence, and human value.

We will no longer treasure managers who continue to divide, to separate, and to polarize. Instead, our new leaders will be *integrators*, skilled in human synthesis and mutuality of intent and effort. Only integrators will achieve mutually beneficial results.

The new business culture is evident among entrepreneurial companies today, where flexibility and maneuverability dominate fixity and steadfastness. Other companies that learn from entrepreneurs will quickly trim their concepts and scaffolding to increase their capabilities. Entrepreneurs aren't successful because they have the best ideas or the greatest intelligence, but because they possess the agility to pursue fleeting opportunity and are lean enough to survive the chase. They can succeed because they are not tied to the legacy of the past: massive capital investment, ingrained management approaches, and obsolete tools and techniques. Their efforts are almost always new, and because they are new they have been created to embody the new culture and to treasure the new values. These are the efforts most aligned with the concept of change, for they are being forged in the white-hot furnace of business-change: today's business climate.

In this climate we will continue to take less and less for granted. Fixed variables are the relics of the past, and nostalgia is beneficial only when it sharpens our awareness of the difference between the past and the present. Because less will be taken for granted, our managers will have to more frequently contrive "mental gathering points," selected reference points at which all members of a project team are allowed to regroup, synchronize their intentions, and recognize a set of mutual accomplishments and goals. Project managers need to coalesce the raw material of their efforts not only at the beginning of a project, but periodically throughout the life of the project, and they need to align not only forces and things but also concepts, energy, and understandings. Again, project managers must be creators and ensurers of *sustained mutuality*.

The new business culture will also favor the quick, the rapid, and the immediate. This increases our dependence on the project mode of work, for projects surpass operations in this regard. They can be marshalled almost instantaneously and implemented with little cost and a minimum amount of time. Toffler touches upon the project model and the matrix (a combination of project-based and functionally based structures) in two of his stunning works, *Future Shock* and *The Third Wave*. In *The Third Wave*, he tells how the project "helps the organization respond to different, quickly changing circumstances. . . . But," he adds, "it also actively subverts centralized control" (1980, p. 259).

Project orientations allow us to *capture* opportunity, while subsequent operations allow us to *exploit* what we have captured. As exploitation times become shorter with change, and capture becomes dependent on alert and mobile management, the abilities to listen and to move quickly become more valuable. The business culture of tomorrow, then, will involve more frequent and more urgent pursuit. And the project, the *energy pulse*, is ideally created to meet that need.

As change becomes more apparent and active, and as company managements recognize the impetus change gives to project efforts and skills, we will see more managers shifting from operations to projects. Even the most operationally entrenched managers will have to encounter and accomplish project tasks more frequently than ever before. The line between projects and operations will begin to blur, and the distinctions will eventually evaporate, for most work will be viewed as project work. As work becomes "projectized," so shall managers.

This being the case, it is best to become acquainted with project skills and project management tenets, no matter what our present alignment may be. We will all need them. If you are going to profit in change, you will profit as some sort of project manager.

The essence of project managers is cohesion. Project managers provide this by acting as organizational "glue," and they exert a strong directing influence upon what they help to bind together. This includes the frequent use of and referral to plans, benchmarks, standards of accomplishment, and temporary achievements, as well as those "mental gathering points" that ensure periodic synchronicity. *Cohesion* and *direction* will replace the old operational needs of *drive* and *efficiency*.

Project managers must be the guardians of plans and of the integrity of objectives, while operationally oriented counterparts are needed to safeguard the productive capacity: the machines, line, or process. The new manager will most often exhibit irreverence for scaffolding, technique, and tradition, whereas the manager in the past defended and reinforced these qualities. In each project experience, the new manager will seek to quickly find and harness the affective essence of the project combination. In contrast, the essence of an operation is fairly obvious to its managers, who seek only to squeeze more and more incremental value from it (to achieve optimization).

The position of project manager is by its nature both tenuous and demanding. No project manager has value without a project, and each demonstrates no strengths except through the project effort. Moreover, project managers cannot hide behind a particular process, concept, or technique. The position of project management is perishable and must be constantly renewed. With operations, management value is embedded in the operational process once synchronization and optimization are attained. The project manager, tomorrow's manager, will have value embedded only in himself or herself. To the degree that this confidence is deserved, it will be acknowledged.

Project managers will seek to create their own policies and rules, to create their own procedures and methods, rather than to comply with those established by others. Project-oriented managers, because of their twin drives for expediency and pragmatism, will value only methods that contribute, that work. They will shun the rest as burdens or obstacles. They should be judged by their resourcefulness and adaptation, in contrast to operational managers of the past, who were punished when they exhibited these traits but rewarded for strict compliance.

In the end, project managers will reap the rewards or penalties of their own embedded capital and that which they nurture in others. They will not be able to depend on fixed assets or scaffolding, nor to cherish attached capital, as is so often done in operational settings. Their challenge will be to transcend differences and limitations rather than to depend on presumed fixity. If they do this successfully, they will become the magicians of the new business world, the project-oriented world of work.

Developing Contrasts

To enhance our appreciation of the fundamental differences between projects and operations, we can contrast their expectations—what they require of us as a price for our allegiance:

Operations Demand that We:	*Projects Demand that We:*
Use them repetitively.	Create and abandon them at will.
Bring opportunity to them.	Use them to pursue opportunity.
Harness similarity.	Harvest diversity.
Let them define expectations.	Let them achieve expectations.
Steer the phenomenon of change.	Steer through or around the phenomenon of change.
Wrap the work around the tools.	Wrap the tools around the work.
Chain people to the process.	Chain the process to people.

The Prices and Risks of Managing Projects, Not Operations

Nothing in this chapter should be construed to diminish the principles of operational management or to suggest that these will no longer be needed. Operational orientations and skills have created the business climate and bounty which most industrialized nations now enjoy, and they will be needed far into the future. What is implied, however, is that, given the nature and emerging awareness of change, the significance of operational models and behavior will diminish, and that of project-oriented approaches will increase.

People who agree with the notion of project suitability and strength in times of change should be aware of the cultural changes it brings and the management ramifications involved. Most of these have been presented in this chapter. In terms of risk and price, however, a few need amplification.

One price, at least to some managements, of a shift to project work is the constant state of organizational flux it requires. We cannot simply reorganize one time and hope this will change our company from a functional, operating organization to a project-sensitive one. Project organizations need to be constantly created, modified, and destroyed. This is often done in concert with modifications and reorganizations on the functional side of the company, where operations occur. Reshaping of project organizations is not done in a vacuum, for it commonly involves movement of people and groups across project-operations borders. Although various forms of matrix organizations have been contrived to facilitate this transition, "tension" is still the best word we can use to describe it.

Process-dependent, technique-addicted, or specialty-limited managers will not be comfortable with the new project environment, just as they are uncomfortable with other aspects of change. Most of the demands of this environment will run counter to their skills and proclivities. Managers who cannot make the attitudinal shift to the new business culture will have to be reassigned to scarcer operational settings, or they will become handicaps to our adaptability.

Executive managers will need to sharpen their own project-related skills—to enhance their ability to harness and nurture strong personalities, independent managers, and creative and innovative pragmatists. Such people are extremely difficult to orchestrate, and simple reliance on procedures or convention will never suffice. Project managers, we must remember, love to create and hate to comply. They will not follow unless they are led. To harvest the bounties they bring, our executive management must reshape its own values and abilities in view of change. Sometimes this price is too high for them.

Project work requires *agility of pursuit* and *agility of perspective* as well. This means we must constantly shift our attention, focus our vision, tune our listening, and most important, reshape our understanding. Frequent reestablishment and modification of view and attitude is difficult for many of us. By our natures, we prefer fixity. Unfortunately, change does not allow us this luxury.

Projects require unique views as well as unique efforts. They exist in and for change, and change affects not only our conversion processes and our particular company attitudes and cultures, but the entire fabric of business enterprise, the culture of the business world. The emergence of projects is but one aspect of this new culture. It affects not only that which surrounds us, but ourselves as well, our group and individual identities and values. To some, this reshaping is painful and frightening. To managers attuned to change, it is exciting, challenging, and very rewarding.

10

Changing the Way
We Think

Remodeling management values

*Everything has changed, except our way of
thinking.*

ALBERT EINSTEIN, 1945

*Systematic research can teach us much. But
in the end we must embrace—not dismiss—
paradox and contradiction, hunch,
imagination, and daring (though tentative)
synthesis.*

ALVIN TOFFLER, 1980

Throughout the preceding chapters we have taken a long and concentrated look at change as it exists and as we respond to it. We have examined both the phenomenon and its effects, and described how we need to change our business objectives and activities to better suit both—to better fit the changing world of today and tomorrow. In so doing, we have created a conceptual outline of the new business ethic, culture, and attitude, and have described the new business manager, the one who will survive and thrive in the dynamically different future.

In short, we have explored how change affects what we see and what we do. We must now address change as it affects a much broader, more intangible, and more subjective aspect of management: our values. Knowing how change influences *what we see* and *what we do*, now we must explore how it influences *what and how we think*.

Taken to heart, a new consciousness of change will cause us to abandon old values and to embrace newer, more relevant ones. At the highest levels of appreciation, we will begin to value the broad, expansive, and diverse and to relinquish the narrow, restrictive, and uniform. We will treasure difference, motion, and the unexpected rather than sameness, stability, and predictability. A deepening appreciation of change brings a higher value to flexibility and adaptation, to awareness and understanding of our conditions, and a lesser value to fixity of purpose or process. It means that we must recognize and even participate in the evolution, growth, and unfolding of our business environments and cultures; that our perception and skills must likewise evolve and grow, expanding with change rather than stagnating or contracting in defiance of it.

As our perceptive and manipulative skills broaden and become more articulate, so will our management effect. For even though change itself is often erratic and unpredictable, our journey through changing times can be guided by reason and intuition, making us its willing passengers rather than its victims. Our goal, then, is not to synchronize specific models or methods in some sort of permanent cadence with change, for this is impossible, but to synchronize our values with the notion of change itself.

To achieve management values consistent with an ever-changing world means we must change those values and be prepared to change them again and again. This is how today's manager becomes the *manager in change*—the manager whose values and attitudes are in harmony with the phenomenon and who avoids the dissonance that change creates for others.

Let us begin by briefly identifying those elements of the management perception and mix that we will value more as we become more attuned to change, and those which will diminish in importance. By applying these to our work environments, we will find that we have optimized *ourselves* instead of simply our processes and tools. Once done, we can then examine a new set of management values, a set of concepts and attitudes more closely synchronized with a changing world.

What We Will Value More

As we become more attuned to change throughout our organizations, we will begin to encourage generalized perceptions and general skills rather than their narrower counterparts. We will promote transferable knowledge and transcending skills, those which can be applied under a variety of differing circumstances. We will encourage loyalty, but not loyalty to technique, process, or organization. Instead, we will want our employees and managers to be loyal to the goals of our work and to the benefits (not the features) of our products. These goals and benefits transcend time and escape its destruction. We will value adaptable approaches and expedient methodology. Proximity of management will be a highly treasured condition, and all telemetry or control scaffolding will be suspect in and of itself—having value only when it increases management proximity without distorting, corrupting, or delaying it. We will place a very high premium on the ability to synthesize and bring disparate forces and potential together, congratulating those who unify others in order to achieve more and more project-specific goals and mutual accomplishments.

Project-oriented managers will become more valuable to us, as will those who know why and how to listen, to watch, and to feel for change. They will be able to plan quickly, organize immediately, and pursue fleeting opportunity with agility and urgency. This urgency is what change demands, for, if we agree with Toffler, we are entering an "accelerative economy" in which "in engineering, in manufacture, in research, in sales, in training, in personnel, in every department and branch of the corporation the same *quickening of decision-making* can be detected" (italics added; 1980, p. 230).

Managers in change will define themselves as what they *can do* rather than what they *have done* in the past. Among their meritable traits will be creativity, imagination, confidence, and independence of discrete methods, machines, or circumstances. Their capital will be portable, embedded in their characters rather than attached to specific conversion processes or equipment. We will reward them for multiple accomplishments, for succeeding without the crutches of rules or rote procedures, and for the ability to transcend mistakes as well as differences. And in order to survive in change and to nurture in others the ability to survive in change, we will have to be prepared to encounter both mistakes and differences with great frequency.

Optimizing Ourselves, Not Just Our Work

As the new managers confront new and changing business settings, they will learn very quickly that reliance on external tools and techniques is not sufficient for success. Whereas managers of the past focused attention on *things*, managers of the future will focus on *people*. They will appreciate the vulnerability of things to change and the ability of people to transcend change. This is why they have begun, and will continue, to see value added in themselves as more important than value added in things. They will recognize that the limitations to optimization are not in its principle, but in its object. They will begin to optimize themselves, and not their work.

They will do this in a number of ways. First, they will put aside the need to divide labor, synchronize processes, fix variables, specialize skills, and perfect methods. Instead they will invest in soft properties, soft process links, and flexible and pivoting controls. These all make a business more responsive and adaptive, although they do not afford "perfection" in any one business aspect.

Optimization in light of change will take on an entirely different connotation, not *refinement* but *responsiveness*. Equipment and tools will no longer be the sole subjects of optimization; people and ideas will be included.

To increase our management optimization, we will give ourselves more freedom to adapt and will acquire the ability to adapt often. We will seek and build enduring qualities, not temporary skills, and we will ferret out change targets so that we will be less susceptible to the ravages of change. The restrictive scaffolding which we have used both for perception and for control will be dismantled. Its replacement will be variably focused, moving, simple telemetry, giving the changeable view and affording rather than perverting proximity.

The new manager in change will be lean and agile, not encumbered with the accoutrements of sight and manipulation but endowed with the enduring qualities of perception and control, and constantly looking for ways to leverage and to encourage the development of these qualities among others. Human optimization will not cease with the individual, then, but will pass through each of us to others, as we seek to propagate adaptability and to nourish the adaptive. We will nurture embedded capital rather than simply extracting that which is attached.

The Prices and Risks of a New Optimization

This new view of optimization, altered from a focus on attached qualities to a valuing of potential, will require a price and a confrontation with risk. By reducing the importance of external value—value attached to machines, processes, and fixed conditions—optimization will require placing values squarely on the human side of every management equation. It will increase the importance of the individual manager and diminish the importance attached to the company, the organization, or the position to which one may be temporarily assigned. It will focus our attention on the whole person, not just selected affects or restricted activity. People who shun this spotlight do not belong on tomorrow's management stage.

Performing well in change means performing for others, and performing under less than ideal circumstances with skills often extemporaneous and unpracticed. We will require our new managers to assume leadership and to manage by leading, through proximity, and with internally derived values. This is a much greater charter than measurement of and control over others, and it is a charter many of today's managers will not or cannot accept. Neither will managers be able to associate only with their own kind, for the force of change is egalitarian, breaking down barriers of status, position, and distance between the manager and the "managed." A new intimacy, with which many of us may be uncomfortable, is needed. Along with this intimacy comes the need to trust others, to delegate not just responsibility but authority—and authority in the future will seldom be as constrained and limited as it is today.

Managers in change must constantly renew proximity and reestablish the basis for trust. They cannot rest on past accomplishments nor hide behind yesterday's success or the methods and tools of today. Managing in change requires continuous testing and performance of our skills and attitudes. As we optimize our skills and approaches in order to ride the tide of change, we will begin to recognize that our ticket must be purchased not just at the start of the journey, but all along the way. This is because *adaptation*, the new optimization, is a journey in itself and not simply a destination. The development of change-sensitive management values is itself a process and not merely a new condition.

The New Management Values

The new values of management will be constantly evolving. Some will develop faster than others, and some will manifest themselves through concrete action and tangible differences, while others will develop slowly, detectable only through subtlety. Depending upon the company, and upon the business process and its viability in the future, some values will become more prevalent than others and some will become much more managerially significant. Regardless of how they take hold, there is no question that the inventory of management values we will see in the future will be stocked and depleted by change. No doubt it will include some or all of the following:

1. *A concern for enrichment rather than optimization.* As a direct result of acknowledgment of the value of people and the need to adapt before we can perfect, we will expand our notion of optimization to include much more than process or tool refinement. We will want to enrich secondary and indirect dimensions of the management effect, and to promote the development of potential attributes in addition to those we can harvest today.

2. *A higher regard for the richness of people and a fully developed respect for their nature and potential.* Virtually everything we can now see and touch in our business enterprise will vanish or change, given enough time. The only exception will be people. They will remain the vehicle and the object of all that we do. They are our most adaptive and flexible resource.

3. *A concern for planting as well as reaping.* The successful businesses of tomorrow are developing the ability to be successful today. Potential is the key to change, and nurturing business cultures will be able to reproduce potential long after it has been depleted by extractive cultures.

4. *An awareness of the peripheral or tangential rather than exclusive interest in the direct.* Change neither begins nor remains within the confines of our limited perception apparatus. It moves in and out of our fields of vision. To appreciate it and to become aware of its imminent effects, we must expand our perception to account for all that occurs, not simply what is within the boundaries of our control. We must destroy or transcend the limits of and barriers to our perception in order to avoid sensory prejudice.

5. *An emphasis on discovery, on creating rather than simply appropriating or extracting.* Our cultures must welcome the prospectors as well as the miners of business opportunity. If we punish creativity, we punish our strongest response to change, and we limit ourselves to only that which we can do today.

6. *Treasuring the power of synthesis, of bringing together rather than dissecting or separating.* Although change often seems to rend apart that which exists, synthesis creates and binds together that which is needed. This makes it a perfect antidote for the damage of change, and a tonic for those wishing to capitalize upon changing events.

7. *A search for the general rather than the specific, for factors which transcend rather than limit.* We can no longer afford a singular march toward specialization but must embrace the general view, the induced idea, and the encompassing effort.

8. *Recognizing the value of independence, freedom, and adaptability of approach.* Those who are addicted to tools, methods, or concepts do not make good discoverers of alternatives or inventors of the pragmatic. Only those among us who realize the limitations of *what we have* are able to pursue the attainment of *what we need.* And our needs constantly change.

9. *Understanding the richness of diversity, knowing that difference is infinite in dimension.* If we don't perceive diversity, in all its shapes and sizes, we will not be able to adapt to diverse conditions or employ different tools to deal with them. The manager who confines difference to the limits of his or her own measure is living in a linear, one-dimensional world. We cannot confine change as neatly as we confine our ability to perceive it.

10. *An appreciation of change as a fluid, evolving process.* Life is a continuum, and so are the active agents within it. We may rely on fixed, discrete models of life or of our business entities and effects, but we must remember these are only contrivances to helping us understand and measure specific aspects. Change may be represented by a series of steps, but it is by no means composed of any discrete series. It is elusive and shapeless. It moves, even though our detection of its movement is possible only through comparison of moved stages, of "representative elements."

11. *A willingness to admit to and accommodate incurred change.* Not all change is of our making, and not all significant change is just that which we plan or control. Even though we focus our attention on the induced effect, we must not ignore the rest, nor the noise and penalties that we didn't bargain for when we intervened.

12. *A growing need for confidence in ourselves.* Change causes us to question reliance on things and to intensify reliance on ourselves. We can transcend change even when our tools, techniques, and temporary postures fall before it. To be a manager in change requires more than using changing tools to meet changing needs. We should not be so dependent on temporary contrivances that meet situationally dependent needs. These too will pass. We must remain.

13. *An appreciation for resourcefulness and expediency.* These twin attributes are critical to the new manager, who must value intelligence and reason over simple knowledge of facts. Facts change, impressions are modified, and understandings fade. Intelligence and reason are always needed, no matter what changes.

14. *Valuing the potential of an idea, an approach, or an individual.* We must stop pricing ideas, approaches, and people according to

their present exchange value, and must realize that potential is priceless. The seeds of today might make excellent grain when milled, but they provide generations of sustenance when planted.

15. *Recognizing that attitude and awareness are more important management characteristics than experience or position.* With the proper attitude and awareness, our managers can evolve with change and become well adjusted to it; without them, all the experience and titles in the world are superfluous.

16. *Isolating and strengthening the affective essence.* Although the need for pragmatic, applied results often thwarts our pursuit of the affective essence, we should not abandon it. The affective essence of our management effort is what will pass through the partitions of time; the *affectations* will drop away. The more closely we can define this essence, the better we can safeguard it and carry it through change untouched. It is the wheat we want to take with us, not the chaff.

17. *Constant consideration of alternatives.* There is always a better way to do something, and change often makes what fails today viable in the future. Alternatives of process, tools, sources, and markets make us less susceptible to change and more flexible to meet changing needs and conditions. We should never discount out of hand those alternatives that may seem oblique, exotic, or unconventional, nor those too simple to merit attention. As with architectural design, less is sometimes more. Elegance and simplicity transcend change better than complexity or intricacy.

18. *Acknowledging the wisdom and courage of release or abandonment.* Far from being a fault, the recognition that something is unsuitable and its subsequent abandonment are prerequisites to passage through time. Managers who insist on keeping that which will not make the transition are dooming themselves and their companies to the past. Tenacity and fervor, when applied to transient technique or apparatus, are undeserved and should be punished. It is often wiser to admit defeat, unsuitability, or failure than to continue it simply as a result of blind dedication. The new manager will have to know when to let go.

19. *Valuing timeliness and adequacy of response.* To respond at less than optimum levels is better than not to respond at all. Mobility and deployment of resources let us pursue and exploit fleeting opportunity, which is the only opportunity we will see in times of change. We should judge a manager's action in this regard by considering its timeliness and adequacy rather than the sheer magnitude of each response. We should reward managers for knowing when and in what direction to jump, rather than punishing them for not jumping far enough.

20. *Balancing command with control.*   When we speak of adaptability, reason, and understanding, we are describing the "control" side of management intervention rather than the power element paralleling its use. The manager in change must be able to balance these two features of the management effect—to balance force with intelligence, power with recognition, action with discrimination, and intervention with control. This is the crux of articulated management, that best suited to the future. The rest is brute motion. When we judge managers in change, we will judge not only their power but their aim as well.

The Bottom Line

Business professionals are distinct from others in their deductive insistence, in their constant demands for the result, the payoff, the bottom line of any theory, conjecture, or analysis. We value the pursuit of knowledge in and of itself, but we also want to apply what we've learned to the productive enhancement of our personal and social conditions. We want to put our knowledge to work. This is as true for change as for any other subject.

When we attempt to summarize the business lessons of change, we fail if we only package them into a few or even many discrete "messages." Although some lessons have been presented here, there are surely many others, and there can be many different interpretations based on specific companies, markets, or business niches. No analysis can pretend to address all these variables sufficiently.

What can be done here, however, is to develop the beginning of a new appreciation of the phenomenon of change—a new awareness with some relevance to what we do, see, and think in the context of business.

Explaining change to someone who has never experienced or appreciated its aspects would be much like explaining color to a person who sees only black-and-white images. Color cannot be fully explained, analyzed, or proved—it must be seen. So it is with change. But we cannot see change frequently enough to appreciate its diverse nature or its ephemeral qualities. We must experience it.

With a new appreciation of change, however, we can begin to see the elements of color in an otherwise black-and-white picture, for change is the continuous painter of our world, who uses unexpected strokes and achieves new and more varied effects—even colors we have never seen before. We might be able to survive with a stationary concept of the business world, living in black-and-white tones, but we can never appreciate the color and texture of our new, evolving world unless we can both see and appreciate the flowing strokes of change.

This, then, is the challenge of change and the new measure of management acuity: to look upon change and see patterns where others see only turbulence, to hear music when others sense only noise, and to derive meaning from what, to the uninitiated, appears only as chaos. Those who can accomplish this feat will profit as today's prophecies are played out. The rest will simply be overwhelmed.

Bibliography

Berman, Morris: *The Reenchantment of the World*, Bantam, New York, 1984.

Boorstin, Daniel J.: *The Discoverers: A History of Man's Search to Know His World and Himself*, Random House, New York, 1983.

Branden, Nathaniel: *Honoring the Self*, Bantam, New York, 1985.

Durant, Will: *The Story of Philosophy*, Washington Square Press, New York, 1953.

Dyer, Gwynne: *War*, Crown, New York, 1985.

Eiseley, Loren: *The Star Thrower*, Times Books, New York, 1979.

Ferguson, Marilyn: *The Aquarian Conspiracy*, Tarcher, Los Angeles, 1980.

Fromm, Erich: *The Sane Society*, Holt, Rinehart & Winston, New York, 1955.

Galbraith, John Kenneth: *The Affluent Society*, Houghton Mifflin, Boston, 1969.

Gilbreath, Robert D.: *Winning at Project Management: What Works, What Fails, and Why*, Wiley, New York, 1986.

Green, Mark, and John F. Berry: *The Challenge of Hidden Profits*, Morrow, New York, 1985.

Gunter, P. A. Y. (ed.): *Bergson and the Evolution of Physics*, University of Tennessee Press, Knoxville, 1977.

Mills, D. Quinn: *The New Competitors*, John Wiley, New York, 1985.

Naisbitt, John: *Megatrends*, Warner Books, New York, 1982.

Peters, Thomas J., and Robert H. Waterman, Jr.: *In Search of Excellence—Lessons from America's Best-Run Companies*, Harper & Row, New York, 1982.

Rifkin, Jeremy, and Ted Howard: *Entropy: A New World View*, Viking, New York, 1980.

Skinner, Wickham: *Manufacturing: The Formidable Competitive Weapon*, John Wiley, New York, 1985.

Thomas, Lewis: *The Lives of a Cell: Notes of A Biology Watcher*, Viking, New York, 1974.

Thoreau, Henry David: *Walden*, New American Library, New York, 1964.

Toffler, Alvin: *The Third Wave*, Morrow, New York, 1980.

Yeats, William Butler: "Among School Children," from *Immortal Poems of the English Language*, Oscar Williams (ed.), Washington Square Press, New York, 1965.

Index

About the author

Robert D. Gilbreath is director of advanced practices for
Theodore Barry & Associates, a national management con-
sulting firm. He advises governments and corporations on
change management and emerging issues. He has lectured extensively and led intensive executive seminars on leading-
edge management strategies and techniques throughout the
United States and around the world, having presented 150
sessions in more than 15 countries from Japan to Singapore,
Finland, Switzerland, and the United Kingdom. This is his
third book dealing with executive issues and business opportunities.